BROWN ROOTS

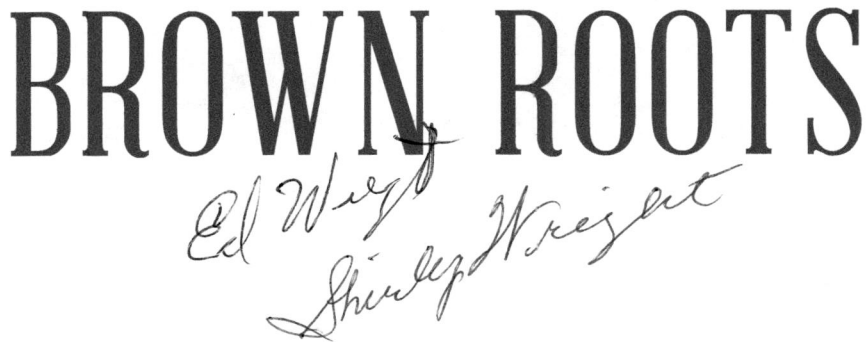

ANTHOLOGY
BLANCHE BROWN WRIGHT
AND FAMILY

EDWARD WRIGHT

authorHOUSE®

AuthorHouse™
1663 Liberty Drive
Bloomington, IN 47403
www.authorhouse.com
Phone: 1 (800) 839-8640

Published by AuthorHouse 09/29/2018

ISBN: 978-1-5462-6236-7 (sc)
ISBN: 978-1-5462-6235-0 (e)

Print information available on the last page.

This book is printed on acid-free paper.

Contents

Foreword

My wife, Shirley Wright, began this book by recording, then transcribing, Blanche Brown Wright and Mary Cecil Park Brown as they recalled their lives over the years. Both were south Texas pioneers whose lives are worth remembering. Three Brown brothers; Les, Paul and Bernard, represent the best our country has to offer. Their sacrifices during World War Two should be known.

With the contributions and help of Elizabeth Brown Alexander and her daughter Alyson Dubler, and the coaching of my son Tim, we offer this anthology for family and friends.

Edward Wright (Tony)

Vollentine Dogtrot House

Charley Crossed the Leona

Charley crossed the Leona and rode up the 50-foot high bank in the shade of the oak and pecan trees, and saw family gathered in the front yard. Uncle Jake's house, at the edge of Batesville…50 yards from the river… was noisy with kids. They had brought chairs out from the house for the women—Aunt Molly, Lora, his sister-in-law, and his elder sister, Ida, who was trying to arrange the children on the front steps.

"We're having a picture taken," said his brother, Gid, standing next to his brother-in-law, John, and Uncle Jake. Cousin Dave stood by the porch rail, rolling a Bull Durham cigarette.

"You're just in time, Charley," he said.

"Naw," grinned Charley. "You don't want me in it; I'm all sweaty and dirty. Still got my chaps on and all."

"Just get off your horse and get with David on the porch rail," said Uncle Jake. "Everybody be still. Take the picture," he told the man with the tripod-mounted camera.

Picture taking was a serious business in 1900. They'd dressed the kids in their finery for the occasion, and it would probably be another ten years before another photo was taken. Charley was the only one who grinned for the camera. But, Charley enjoyed himself more than most. He enjoyed being with family and friends…enjoyed whatever he was about.

Aunt Molly and Uncle Jake had come west from Fayette County years before to settle the land. They built a typical house for the time…two big rooms under a shingle roof, separated by a dogtrot where a table sat. It had a loft reached by steps from the front porch. The whole structure rested on mesquite posts and sat four feet off the ground. A chicken-wire fence around the porch kept the kids from falling off. Inside the main room, a large fireplace was used for cooking and heating in cold weather. Cooking and washing took place under an arbor in back…not far from the windmill and its water tap. A two-hole outhouse sat 75 paces further back.

Charley had come to Frio County in 1898. He and his two brothers drove a herd of the family's cattle to the new ranch they had traded for their farm near Halletsville, in Lavaca County. Charley's father, Barney, quickly saw to it that a substantial house was erected…enough room to accommodate his large family of seven grown children.

It wasn't long before the local social scene included most of Charley's siblings…picnics and dances being the principal entertainment for the teens and twenty-somethings of the era. Charley was built like his father and taller than his brothers. He frequently assumed a leadership role even though he wasn't the eldest in the family. He liked to laugh and got away with teasing others because of his ready smile.

In 1899 Charley asked for and was allowed to develop a ranch on land his mother, Margaret Ann, had inherited in Zavala County. The property began on the Leona River just east of the village of Batesville and bordered the farm of his Aunt Mollie and Uncle Jake Vollentine. The Vollentines had come out from Halletsville years before and built a dogtrot house a few yards west of the river. It was Charley's first opportunity to operate on his own. He'd spent some time at St. Louis College in San Antonio, but did not see the need to graduate. Although Uncle Jake farmed the adjacent property, Charley was determined to be a cattleman.

The first year he had cleared land for a house, and dug a well on his new place. The new house would someday have a kitchen and dining room, two bedrooms on the west side, with a porch running the full length of the east side. At first it had only one long room, with a partition for a kitchen. Unpainted, the house would stand on mesquite posts about two feet off the ground.

A two-holer outhouse sat 40 paces away from the back door.

A large mesquite tree grew on the north side of the house and provided shade on laundry days, or for the days when animals were butchered. A blacksnake resided under the house, keeping away rats and other rodents, but not the ever-present rattlesnakes. Charley saw to it that many cats were around for that.

A large one-story tin barn with wooden floor went up in the early years. It had extended sheds on either side for a shaded pigpen, saddle and harness storage, and a covered milking area. Charley literally had to tame the land. The very first night he came to the place he'd left the cattle to graze near the river, and hobbled the horse and mules. When it was good and dark he bedded down in the buckboard bed, noticing clouds had covered the stars. Sometime in that dark night he felt a motion of the wagon. Something was walking up the tongue, and it was big! He'd left his rifle in its scabbard on his saddle and it was on the ground. Charley jumped up and yelled, "Heya!" He waved his arms, and then felt the animal jump off the tongue. It was quiet for a while, but Charley elected not to get out of the buckboard. All night he sensed the animal around, but couldn't see it in the dark. He didn't sleep. The next morning he saw panther tracks all around. The cattle and horses were okay, but Charley slept with his rifle thereafter.

Unlike the live oak forests around Halletsville where he was raised, the brush country in Zavala County houses whitebrush and guajilla, prickly pear and mesquite trees. There were plenty of pecan and oak trees along the creeks and rivers, but the flint and caliche hills didn't hold much grass. Charley's inheritance wouldn't feed many cattle per acre either. He would have to scramble to get as much off the land as he could. Fortunately his Father had surplus funds, so he could share to get things started. Wagon loads of cedar posts were purchased from the hill country. Barbed wire fences had to be put up to keep the animals in. He did one pasture at a time with help from the native Mexican people whose ancestors had been in the area for centuries. As the cattle multiplied, he'd fence a pasture, seventy or eighty acres at a time, then more as time went by.

He brought in twenty-five Mexican goats, letting them out in the mornings and bringing them back to pens at night. Predators killed so many that in the second year he hired Juan Nava, an experienced herder who lived at the edge of Batesville. Juan came at daybreak, stayed all day in the brush with the goats, and then walked home each night, seven days a week. He'd been a goat herder all his life and had a crippled hand from snakebite. He talked to his dogs, who were the real minders of the goats. Goats multiplied faster than cattle, and there was a ready local market for cabrito.

Charley had learned beekeeping early, and the brush around the ranch provided excellent honey. He added aviaries in several places around the property.

Of course, he needed pens; and land had to be cleared for a hayfield. Three locals were hired to cut and trim the mesquite trees and brush alongside the Batesville-to-Friotown road. It wasn't really a road, merely a cart path that wound through the hills in an east/west direction. The field was cleared and mesquite limbs used to build six-foot tall corrals, stout enough to hold the toughest bull or the wildest horse.

A wooden tank, mounted twenty feet in the air, would someday provide enough water to sustain animals and people through a buried plumbing system. It fed water troughs, and a faucet above a wooden sink (carved from a mesquite stump) located in the house, but at first water had to be fetched from the dug well.

All this work was ahead of Charley when the picture was taken in the Vollentine's front yard. He rarely left the property, learning about the land, the cattle and the area, returning to the Covey Chapel area of Frio County and the family home only on holidays and special occasions.

In the few years since coming to the County, Bernard (Barney), Charley's father, prospered. A strong Catholic, Barney contributed land for a Catholic Church and cemetery to serve the people of the Covey Chapel area where they lived. As the principal landowner he quickly became a leader in the community, both socially and politically. It was the social activity that brought Charley home.

Bernard Brown 1908

The Covey Chapel area was a lure for Charley—for one thing his family lived there. Social life among the young people usually involved a gathering around a birthday, anniversary or other event.

The Browns had quickly become active and over time, his sister, Viola, introduced him to Mary Cecil Park, a schoolmate her same age. The principal social event among the young set was dancing. Music was provided by a piano, guitar and fiddle. The young folk would travel miles to gather for dancing and socializing, sometimes riding all night to return home. It was four hours on horseback to Todos Santos Lake where Mary Cecil lived, and further to his family's home, so Charley did not have many opportunities for socializing or courting.

He found time during Christmas in 1904. He and "Cecil" were married in May of 1905 in Frio County. Their honeymoon was a trip to the ranch near Batesville.

Mr. & Mrs. C. A. Brown

Mary Cecil was born by Todos Santos Lake in Frio County, the daughter of Billy Park and Mary Elizabeth Mudd. As there were no publicly funded schools in the area, her education consisted of privately supported schools which ran for a few months, then closed until more money could be raised. Her cousin, Si Park, who had attended Sam Houston State College, was the teacher. Cecil later attended school in San Antonio, living with her Aunt Annie Congdon.

Mary Cecil's father had been a trail driver in the old days, worked wherever he could as a cowhand, brand inspector and helper on his older brother's ranch. But Mary Cecil, the eldest girl in her family, had received a thorough education as a housekeeper. Charley had finished the two years at St Louis University in San Antonio, so both were well equipped for life together in south Texas.

There was corn nearing harvest in the field when their buckboard arrived with all Cecil's clothes, furniture, seed for a garden, staples from sugar to flour—even a yeast starter for bread. The two of them literally started life from scratch. She had a cage of chickens on the back of the wagon, which she released in the new coop Charley had built.

The cattle herd Charley originally brought from Frio County had grown to fifty cows and two bulls. Each spring in the last five years he'd kept the female calves and sold the last year's yearling crop of steers, combining with other ranchers to drive them to market in Uvalde.

Starting with some swarming bees he'd spotted in a mesquite tree near the windmill, he now had four hives going to take advantage of the honey from the guajillo and other blossoms in the area.

As Charley made furniture, Cecil made the house into a home; she quickly took over the chickens, turkeys, guineas and ducks. A garden went in that summer. She cooked for ranch hands and anyone else who dropped in to the remote site.

In February of 1907 Mary Blanche was born—her grandmother, Mary Elizabeth, attending. Eighteen months later a boy, Leslie, was born. Although there were five other children, the two eldest bonded and in their early years were inseparable.

7

Charles, Cecil, Blanche & Les

Blanche shared these years when she was in her late seventies, dictating to her daughter-in-law, Shirley Wright, over many days:

"My earliest memory of a family circle began—Mama and Papa, Brother Leslie and I, affectionately called "Titter" by my lisping brother. (I was the first of seven children). It would seem that I could always talk, but I've been told that my grandfather taught me to say my first word—"moon". And I can remember Pedro, a youth who worked on our ranch teaching me to say "estrella" (star), "papel" (paper), "guajalote" (turkey), and "tecolote" (owl).

You see, Pedro was Jose and Susie's grandson. Old Jose was blind; his good wife, Josie, 'sorta' looked after us all. They lived in one of two huts located beyond our garden fence. In the other hut lived Alcadia and her sons, Pedro and Simon. Simon was younger than I, but older than my brother. I tell you this in order that you understand my role as reporter of any lies told by either Pedro or Simon. My parents believed in honesty and truthfulness at all times. If either of the boys bit me or pulled my hair and denied the deed, I was recognized as setting forth the truth. I was older and had my responsibilities. If one threw sand in the other's face that too was reported. Among my other early duties was seeing to it that neither boy robbed a bird's nest or kept a terrapin penned up too long. Mostly, I recall myself as keeper of the peace, but I do confess to acts of disobedience.

There were some tree stumps in our front yard and Pedro burned them out. The rosy glow of ashes looked as pretty and soft as the rose petals on the climbing roses on our gallery, as our front porch was called. I probably wouldn't have noticed the rosy glow had not Mama warned me not to walk there. I suppose it was the Devil that tempted me. I couldn't resist walking through those ashes barefooted when the first stump was burned. To make it worse, when the second stump was burned, I was tempted and succumbed again. The first time I was scolded and consoled. I had to spend several days sitting with my feet in a pan of water that had baking soda in it. For the second fall from grace, I got paddled in addition to all the above mentioned. I guess Brother was an infant in the arms at the time, since I don't recall his joining me.

Nor did he join me in trying to eat with Viejo, our dog. Viejo did not wish to share with me our table scraps, which I'd been permitted to serve him. To this day I have the scar as evidence of his protest. Mama had warned me. She glued my cheek together with the inner membrane of an egg—our Band-Aid of those days. Fortunately, Viejo bit me before the days of rabies shots and the scar now coincides with a laugh wrinkle. It didn't hurt Viejo either. He lived to be twelve years of age.

And what a private world it was. We were completely isolated from the outside world, or so it seemed. Huge mesquite trees seemed to enclose our world. Daily we roamed in the pastures, perhaps cutting notches in the prickly pear or branding leaves, thereby claiming them as our make-believe cattle. Dusk was the time we played with the sheep and goats, mostly trying to make them pull us in our little wagon.

Sometimes we perched on the roof of our barn to watch the real branding or dipping of cattle. A seldom-used road passed in front of our ranch house. It rarely rained, but when it did, our road became a stream of running water, which drained to the river. We couldn't wait for the rain to stop because then we could go wading. We were always admonished not to fall down and get our clothes wet. Of course, we invariably did. And it wasn't but a few summers before we started falling down purposely. It was such fun wallowing in the gushing water. A hard rain always gave us the urge to go to the outhouse. This meant we were dressed in our slickers and overshoes and could walk in the rain carrying our umbrella. It didn't matter that we had to walk through the chicken yard where the fighting turkey gobbler reigned. We enjoyed seeing all the bedraggled chickens. My brother would lasso the gobbler.

Our outhouse was a very special place. It was a two-holer. The floor was littered with newspapers and Sears Roebuck catalogues. One could get carried away there what with all the cartoons, pictures, etc. Of course, everybody knows that toilet paper had not yet been invented.

The road sometimes produced a passerby about once a month. A lone horseman would ride up, step down and sit a spell. This visitor was in the form of an old man, especially interesting, because he had a deformed foot, the result of a rattlesnake bite. He would help himself to a cool drink of water. Everybody had a canvas-and-toe-sack-covered earthen bucket suspended from the ceiling of his front porch. The public dipper hung on a nail nearby. After taking a drink, one poured any water remaining in the dipper onto the outside of the olla (pot). This kept the contents cool, especially with the water jar swaying in the breeze. This old man had a grown son who sometimes drove by in a wagon. He would be on his way to the small town some three miles away to haul supplies. He, too, would stop to chat—sometimes staying for lunch. In fact, I remember our Mother say that he never knew when to leave.

There came the time when my father decided to have open space in front of our ranch house—land was cleared for an oat patch. Just a few big shade trees were left growing on the area in front of our house.

My Mother had a buggy. She and I could go to town. I always clung to my Mother's skirt if we went into a store. I was as scared as a wild rabbit. I much preferred not leaving the ranch. About the only result of a trip to town that I can recall was that of getting a candy whistle hung in my throat. My mother grabbed me by the ankles, suspended in midair, and beat me on the back until the whistle flew out. And the candy had been so pretty—like a ribbon folded back and forth, with the whistle embedded inside. Well, no more whistles.

One day, a most memorable event took place. Old Susie called us from play to come see what we had! Imagine our astonishment in seeing a tiny, red-haired baby in Mama's arms. What a surprise! We'd never even dreamed of a baby sister. Now, our circle was enlarged. I was four years old and felt quite possessive. My brother started referring to me as "Big Titter". I'll tell you of how she helped spice up our lives, not that we were ever bored.

The size of our family now decreed that we have a surrey. What a beauty it was! It had fringe all around the top. There was the stand for the buggy whip. It had two leather seats. Then it seemed to be time for us to go 'down home.' Down home was my grandparents' farm. In those days to go 'down home' was to take an all-day trip—one that we probably took about twice a year—always if it didn't rain.

We would leave early as we had to cross a river with running water and several dry riverbeds. Each time the back wheels of the surrey had to be tied before we could descend. Once we reached the bottom, the wheels had to be untied in order that the team of horses could pull the surrey uphill. My father generally let us play by the roadside while he was getting the surrey across. We loved this because we enjoyed gathering wildflowers that grew so abundantly. The thistles were very thorny, and they were certainly not fragrant, but they grew in glorious colors—reds, purples and white. Also, we would see deer, javelinas and wild turkeys along the road. At noon we would camp by a tank for our picnic lunch.

On one such trip Mama called us to point out that the object we could barely see on the far side of the tank was our father.

She said, "Look. That's Papa. He's swimming."

"Swimming," we shouted, "that's swimming?"

That was the first time we ever saw anyone else swim. It was then that we realized that we could swim.

After lunch every day when our parents took their siesta, it was our time to make mud pies. There was plenty of clay on our reservoir dump. My brother or I would get a bee-sting on our toes. By submerging our feet in the water the sting hurt less. Finally it happened that in soaking his big toe, Brother fell in the water. Of course, I'd rescue him. One thing led to another. We'd just gotten the habit of falling in purposely—it was so cooling. And we'd learned that I no longer had to sneak into the house for dry clothes for Brother—the sun soon dried his clothes anyhow.

We had been practicing trying to "walk on the water", an idea we had acquired from a picture of "Our Lord Walking <u>on</u> the Water." Crawling on the water had been the best we could do. Not until Mama told us that Papa was swimming that day, did we realize that we could, and had been, swimming, for quite a while.

We loved visiting our grandparents. They grew watermelons, cantaloupes, tomatoes, okra and cucumbers. They cured their own meat. That sausage and smoked bacon cannot be bought in stores today.

We felt so grown up and helpful when sent to gather eggs, feed the chickens, and walk with Grandpa when he went to milk at daybreak. Grandma let me churn; also I was taken around to visit the several tenant families who lived on the place.

Cotton was their main crop. One of our favorite places to play was in the cottonseed room in the barn. Of course, I did once get a cottonseed hung in my nostril, but Grandma soon got it out with a shoe buttonhook. The corncrib was a good place to see scurrying mice, but the cornhusks itched! We had lots of fun with corncobs. And there was the big wrap-around porch. I lost a front tooth there just pushing a bee box until it suddenly stopped when it hit a groove in the floor. Grandma cooked delicious garlic-flavored pinto beans with cornbread. Also, she served us fresh buttermilk. Grandpa had a commissary where the tenant farmers came for supplies. He'd give us an occasional cinnamon stick to chew.

My brother, Leslie, was more a playmate—and one about whom I felt protective. In fact Mama deputized me to help her.

Blanche & Les

My earliest memory pictures Leslie, Simon (old Susie's grandson) and me prowling in the woods. We frequently investigated bird's nests. Mama scolded us, and told us to leave the nests alone. When I saw Leslie and Simon still disturbing bird's nests, I reported to Mom. Leslie denied the deed and was paddled. Again Mom asked me to keep her informed if they did it again. They did! I did! And Mama did!

Before we were of school age, we'd make daily rounds through the pastures gathering mesquite or catclaw wax (our chewing gum) or gathering pitayas in season, or chewing mesquite beans. We'd burn out rats' dens, hunting snake or rats to kill.

In our smoke house lived a big old blue snake. If things got dull, Leslie would tie him to a fishing line, and we'd watch the big snake swim across the reservoir. Then the snake would be yanked back and finally returned to his quarters.

Frequently we built lean-to playhouses of guajillo branches—or sometimes we'd play "combate" with our little Mexican friends--Ida, Paz and Tolin-- using long guajillo sticks for arms. Once we were losing the battle, and we had to fly home so fast that we scraped our baby Hestel's head when we scurried under barbed wire fences as she lay in our wagon. Needless to add, Mama did not approve of our bringing home our baby with forehead scratched and bloody. At least we hadn't abandoned wagon, baby and all!

If we were on friendly terms with our playmates, we would cook outdoors and share our food. They taught us to roast and eat Spanish Dagger bloom stalks, and we'd brew pecan leaves tea or corn cob coffee.

Leslie was a good sport. Once, after the first trip to church that I can remember, Leslie agreed to say Mass. He let me dress him up in Mama's nightgown. He held church in our "off-limits to kids" parlor, unknown to Mama. Leslie, as a priest, spoke fluent Latin mumbo-jumbo while I was his one parishioner.

Once he let me try to give him pierced ears by holding a cricket to his ear lobe.

Every night, after supper, Brother practiced his rodeo skills down in the goat pen. Considering he had only baling wire for harness, I now understand why he could never get that old Billy goat to pull me in the wagon.

It rarely rained, but when it did, we took advantage of the water and swam in the dipping vats. We were allowed to fish in the reservoir whenever we liked, but had to use bent pins for hooks.

Leslie was sometimes a detective—when the thieving wife of one of our workmen came to the windmill to draw water, she'd let the water trickle while she hastily robbed our hens' nests, fig trees, or stole mash from the barn. Leslie would hide on the windmill water tower and, after the thievery, shout at the woman to put back the stolen objects. She finally became so angry she rushed around to tell "Mr. Cholley" who sat there reading the morning paper.

We hastily crawled under the porch from the far side in order to make faces at the tattling woman. Needless to say, she and her husband decided to move to Batesville, and the husband had to commute to work thereafter.

One of Leslie's early cigarettes was made of ground-up flowers (Mexican hat), which grew profusely around the reservoir. But, he gave up that type of tobacco after the first trial resulted in a flare-up with singed eyebrows.

Leslie always knew what he wanted. Papa had hung up some green peanut stalks to dry. Leslie was playing in the barn—a little toddler of 2 or 3 years. Under one of the bushes hanging on a nail was a cowbell with the leather belt hanging within Leslie's reach. To try to get peanuts down, Leslie yanked and yanked until down came cowbell, peanuts and all. The bell nearly cut off his little button nose. I fetched Mama who sent me for an egg and a washrag. She soon glued his wound back in place with the lining of the egg—our early-day scotch tape.

Leslie stuttered when he was little—he couldn't sound his esses. When he was six and about to start school, I drilled him on saying my name so he wouldn't call me Big Titter at school.

In season, there were wild grapes, wild berries, pitahayas and tunas (prickly pear fruit) to gather. I am sure that our fare also included mesquite beans, when the beans were ripe. Catclaw and mesquite gum served as our chewing gum. We made lean-to shanties of guajillo; we cooked frijoles, tortillas and potatoes. We brewed tea of pecan leaves or of senesa (sage). Sometimes we took our dog, "Viejo", and hunted rattlesnakes by burning out rat's nests.

The event in our lives in those days—when the grapes were ripe on the river, the family would saddle up horses and we'd ride down there—all of us—Mama and the kids, sometimes Papa; I guess he went with us in the early days.

Gathering grapes was a family event. We took flour sacks and loaded the grapes in them. You had to stand on the back of the horse on the saddle to reach the grapes because they were hard to get to; they hung on the edge of the river and it was very hard to be tall enough to get to them. Sometimes you could get them from the saddle or climb the vine, whatever. We would balance the bunches of grapes on both sides of the saddle horn. The whole family participated. We'd return with our riches and Mama made jam, jelly and grape juice.

Sometimes we got green grapes for green grape pie—very good—and grape cobblers, a special taste you can't buy in a store.

You didn't go to the store and buy Coca-Cola. If you had a treat, it was either going to be lemonade if you were to have found some lemons in the store, or homemade grape juice. That's what we always had to drink when we camped out or anything—all our play—was grape juice. It was a real luxury to have that grape juice. Mama would boil the grapes and make the juice and then put a cork in the bottle to seal it with wax.

We didn't have ice in those days, you just had cool water. You cooled the grape juice bottle and you thought you were getting something. On the front porch Mama had what we called a milk stand, all metal. It had shelves in it and she could set her milk crocks in on the different shelves. You put water down in the base of it and then a sheet around the outside. You wet it from above, all sides. That made it a cooler. You cooled your milk, butter and anything you wanted cool. That was the closest to a refrigerator we had in those days.

Mama didn't care how long we kept the milk fresh because she couldn't wait for it to sour. She'd skim it for the butter and then take the clabber that was left, put it in a flour sack to drain. That made cottage cheese.

Those carefree days ended when I was seven years old, (Les five, Hestel two, and Paul one). The family moved to Batesville, Texas, in order that my brother and I begin school. Our first day at school was spent looking out the window to be sure that our new house was still in view. Mama had taken us upstairs so we could see the school two oat fields away, but I was still scared we wouldn't find the house. We were terribly shy, not having been around very many people. About the only people who came through the country in those days were occasional cattle-buyers. If we saw anybody riding up to the ranch house, it had been our habit to run hide under a bed until the visitor left the house.

The older children thought we were oddballs. They'd corner us at recess and not let us go until we would "talk Mexican, talk Mexican." We'd just say "Me

Llama" and whatever our name was, so they would let us go. The school had a windmill with a pipe that led down into a hole in the ground. When pulled up, the pipe squirted water. Each child had their own tin drinking cup.

The girl's restroom was a sixteen holer with a barricade in front of it. You entered from one end, but it was all open inside. It was so much bigger than we were used to. Of course, they had Sears and Roebuck catalogs for toilet paper.

We played a game called stealing sticks, (sort of a rough tag game), but soon they made a rule that the girls could not play with the boys. They were put on the other side of the schoolhouse.

In the fifth grade, I couldn't think of anything more boring than playing with just girls. I had a good friend, Ruby Hunt, daughter of the County Judge. (Batesville was the county seat in those days). We would catch the boys on the steps and bump them. We did that till a teacher told us we were not ladies. I was horrified to be told I was not a lady. I learned the hard way you can't play with the boys.

During World War One the girls got headbands. There were ice cream socials on Sundays to raise money, and we saved our peach seed and aluminum wrappers. People saved the foil around packaged cigarettes, although most people smoked Bull Durham, which came in a bag. The peach seeds were used to make some form of acid for poison gas. I was taught to knit a washrag, but mostly we delivered the ice cream that the Red Cross Ladies sold for the war effort.

When Leslie was about 12 years old it was decided he should have his first long pants. When L. Schwartz and Company delivered his new suit, I was the only one to hear knock-knock on the door and secure the package. The other members of the family were in the kitchen. This gave me the inspiration to try on the suit. I dressed up, painted on a sooty mustache, put on Leslie's hat and went out on the front porch and rang the doorbell. This time Leslie heard and rushed to the door. As he opened the door, I barged past him – the astonished Leslie saying "Er–er–er" until he recognized the new suit. He soon upended me and recovered his property—and finally at long last his independence from Blanche.

17

We had a neighbor boy who was a kleptomaniac. The poor fellow broke into our house once when we were off visiting our grandparents. When we got home, I discovered all my pretty hair ribbons were gone—my little trunk lid standing open. I later found those bows stuffed into rat holes in our barn.

At one period in our days living in Batesville, we were able to raise a baby rabbit the workmen at the ranch found. Papa had brought it home in his coat pocket. This baby grew to be a full-grown jack rabbit. It loved to scamper through the house when we let it run. Sometimes we'd chase it with a water gun just to see it stop and knock off the water from its long ears. By tying a cord to the little leather belt we had around its neck, and then nailing the other end to a croquet ball (which is wooden), we were able to let the rabbit run loose in the yard. The croquet ball kept Jackie from escaping through the picket fence. That is until this overgrown imbecile who had stolen my hair ribbons started chasing Jackie. The result was that the string came loose and Jackie ran away, and was never seen again. I can't remember which child owned this pet jackrabbit, but perhaps he belonged to Hestel.

About the nicest play place at our Batesville house was that it was located on several acres of land, bounded on two sides by irrigation ditches bordered by huge pecan trees. The very best area was where several trees were covered with wild mustang grape vines. One huge vine made a perfect swing over the water. We could sit there dangling our feet in the water. We could climb up the grapevines and literally roll high above the ground. In fact, it grew to be quite a feat to run from the house when we heard a car coming, climb the grapevine tree, and be high above the road by the time a car passed beneath. Grape vines were our early day "chupas" (sucking on). We'd heard telephone bark made an excellent smoke. I tried it once after rolling the bark in a piece of newspaper as our washerwoman did with her "Bull Durham." We lighted our cigarettes from the coals under Zenaida's wash pot (where she boiled our clothes). Our cedar bark flamed up almost burning our eye lashes and hair. After that we favored grapevine joints for smokes. They even had a good taste and did not flare up.

I remember that Norma was born while we lived in Batesville because we got to go and stay with Uncle Milton and Aunt Norma on that occasion. Bernard and Jeanne were born when we lived in Uvalde.

Our neighbor, Mr. Pinkham lived across the ditch on the west side of our oat patches (fields). If Mr. P. saw us out gathering pecans from our trees on our side of the ditch, he'd come out and shows us a pecan from the trees on his side of the fence and ditch. He would instruct us to toss over to him any pecans that looked like his sample. Of course, we'd run home and have a good laugh over Mr. Pinkham's pecans. (All the pecans that landed on our side we assumed belonged to us.) Furthermore, pecans were plentiful.

We sometimes took washtubs down to the ditch to try to sail them. It never worked. When we sat in them they became unbalanced.

Another memory I have of our loft and barn is that a skunk came out right about the foot of the ladder. We ran to the house to tell the tale. Uncle Milton happened to be there at the time. He came out and shot the skunk. We were to take off the carcass into the woods and dispose of it. Leslie and I had heard that skunk hides were bringing 25 cents. Brother said he'd skin the skunk if I'd go get the knife. Our sharpest knife, I thought, was a case knife that had been sharpened. Anyhow, we took the skunk down to the bank of the ditch, and Leslie tried manfully to skin it. With the dull knife he had to stand on the body to hold it just to make an incision. The net result that we finally abandoned the idea of selling skunk hides. Leslie tried to wash in the ditch water to no avail. When we went back to the house, Mom met us at the kitchen door and ordered Brother out! He was an undesirable for several days. Mom tried everything— even soaking his shoes and stockings in tomato juice, milk, etc. Nothing worked. Burying was tried, but that did not restore Leslie's Sunday shoes!

When we moved to town, Mama decided that we had to learn to milk the cows. And so Brother was a milker, Mama was a milker, and they decided that I should be a milker. But, I was not a success...the cow would kick the bucket over...my heart wasn't in it.

Aunt Norma had told me that if you never learn to milk the cow, you'll never have to. And I could not—I took her advice to heart and decided I'd be a poor

19

milker. *My fingernails would cut into the cow's tit; she'd kick over the bucket, and we'd lose the milk. Then she wouldn't give down the milk. So it wound up that I didn't have to milk for very long. I'd rather be playing in the hayloft anyway. In Batesville we had a two-story barn, but below were two stalls for cows and a huge garage for the car.*

Batesville was still country living. We had a garden; we had an oat patch. There was the irrigation ditch with the most beautiful grapevine you'll ever see. It had a big swing clear across the ditch. We could sit there and dribble our feet in the water as it rushed by. The grapevines grew on the big pecan and oak trees that grew on the ditch.

I started a school in the fine hayloft we had. I persuaded Papa to make me some blackboards. So, he painted the inside walls of the upstairs part of the barn for blackboards. Mama got me some chalk; I had a rag for an eraser, and we played school. We had plenty of bee boxes for desks. We'd take a bee box, turn it upright on its end, and that made the front desk. You sat on the other one—turned lengthwise—a perfect desk.

I persuaded my classmates to come to school to me—mostly all boys. I don't remember any girl students at all. But, I had a following that were glad to come. I was eight or nine years old at the time. The school lasted every Saturday for two or three years. I taught arithmetic and spelling to anyone who wanted it.

I always knew that I was going to be a teacher, but school ended when an obstreperous boy who lived across the street—a dear friend of mine who was my age—had to be punished. I was very handy with a paddle and went to punish him. He ran from me, skidded on the hay through the hole you slid hay to the cows below; it knocked the breath from him, and I thought he was dead. I don't remember playing school after that.

On Friday afternoons we played baseball in front of our house. All the kids came up there because we had a wide area at the end of the street. We didn't have a real ball. Mama made a fine string ball by sewing the twine back and forth. For a bat we used a board. That ball would go to Jericho. It was so fine.

Baseball got me in trouble with Grandma, or she almost got me in trouble at home, because Papa had gone down to Dilley and was bringing her up to visit us. He stopped downtown in Batesville at the store, and Grandma stayed in the buggy while Papa went in. She overheard one of the boys say, "That ole Blanche Brown knocked a home run right through the hayloft door."

Grandma was aghast that I would do anything so unladylike; first, that I'd be playing with boys and that Mama would let me do it! When she got to the house, Grandma let Mama know what she thought of my unladylike life. Actually, Mama took it with a grain of salt, but she allowed me to continue with the stipulation that I had to sit at the piano for thirty minutes—seemed like a year—before I could join the team. My heart was on the baseball field, but I did my duty. I had to take music two years while we lived in Batesville and then one year in Uvalde before she dismissed me from piano.

We played baseball until we moved to Uvalde, where the girls had P.E., and all girls played softball—with a real ball—no more hardball. If that didn't kill me, it was that we had to pitch underhanded.

Of course, when I went to University we played baseball—hardball (I was a first baseman). We also played basketball, and then volleyball—which I'd never heard of.

We had a fine player piano when we lived in Batesville. When they were young, Papa and Mama loved dancing, and it was customary for the people to come to our house on Saturday nights. Someone would pump the piano, and the grownups and kids would dance. We were too young to be involved, but our home was the center of the social life in Batesville in those days.

I remember at the end of World War One, Papa built a 60'X60' platform in our front yard and gave the returning veterans a ball. Grandma had three cousins (Mudds) who were among the veterans among them. Relatives and friends came from far and wide to participate.

In Batesville, we lived across the street from the School Superintendent, Mr. Wilson, whose wife was my second grade teacher. She was my inspiration to become a teacher. She was from Kentucky, and she talked about the

Cumberland Mountains and the Blue Ridge mountains. I just thought it must be paradise. She was a wonderful teacher.

My rival in school was W.T., whose father always bragged about his smart boy. He had daughters, but the father only bragged about his son, so I vowed to outdo him in school. I had to make a higher grade than W.T. or I would be unhappy. In the end, he and his sisters turned out to be our good friends.

They lived next to an old dug well which was partly filled with debris. We would go there and play in that debris; I remember an abandoned chamber pot we used. We played there till we encountered a live buzzard someone had trapped in that well. Never went there again.

On our property we had an underground storm cellar right outside our kitchen door. We determined there were no snakes in it, and it had a dug bench completely around it. We got an old piece of pipe and made a fireplace and played down there. We were the gathering place for the neighborhood till Mama heard one of the kid's say he came over to play so his Mom could take a nap.

One day, right after World War One, we were playing with our friends in front of the house, when an ace—they called him an ace—flew his plane right over Batesville and landed in our field by the river. We had never seen an airplane before and were paralyzed at the loud noise as it flew so low. Paul ran to the back door and said, "Mama, was that God?" In those days we saw our first car, first telephone, and first plane. The next day, we got to go and see the plane up close; some got to sit in the seat.

During the school year we went to the ranch to pick up eggs and gather figs, whatever, just to be going. But we returned to the ranch each summer. Papa stayed there year round.

Mama prohibited us from swimming in the reservoir at the ranch, unless she was present. In the afternoons, she would nap then go with us for our swim— maybe at 4.00 pm each day. We always said, "Mama, what do you care, you can't swim?" She'd reply, "I'd know where you went down."

In later years, our Sunday afternoon event was going to the dam on the Leona River. Everyone in town met up there. There was a wire strung across the river you could hang on. When Bernard was young he was hanging on the wire and slipped off. If Mama had not seen where he went down, we might have lost him.

One time I was going to teach Mama to swim. She agreed that she'd go in. We waited till nighttime, in the moonlight, in her nightgown—she had no bathing suit. As I took her out she said, "It won't do any good. My heels come up, my head goes down." And sure enough I laid her down—I just knew I could teach her to swim because it was so natural for us. Sure enough, Mama's heels went up and her head went down, and I couldn't hold her. So she got out. And that was the end of my teaching her to swim.

A wooden bed was already part of Papa's bachelor pad when he and Mama married in 1905. It had a mattress of goose feathers from "down east"— meaning that it came with the Brown family when they moved from Lavaca County on or before 1900. A second, more solid cotton mattress was used on top of the goose feather mattress or vice versa, depending on whether it was warm or cold weather season. I suppose we dubbed it "the Rock of Gibraltar" because of its lumps, which developed when the feathers were not evenly distributed.

It was the bed in which the first five Brown children were born. It represented many things to us. I personally think of the cookies I ate in bed as I lay between my parents. Mama always placed water and cookies at our bedside at night. She was trying to break me of sucking my thumb. If she caught me with my thumb in my mouth as I slept, it was yanked out and a cookie was the substitution. And, of course, I'd get thirsty. Then I soon became hooked on cookies—Mom's homemade teacakes. No wonder I was always the chubby type.

At the old ranch house, the Rock of Gibraltar and Mom's treadle sewing machine—a Minneapolis—were the principal pieces of furniture in our middle room window.

After we moved to Batesville, Papa's young ranch hands took partitions out of the old ranch house and it was used for dances. We were too little to go, but dances were a big thing then.

In 1926 Batesville built a new brick schoolhouse. Papa bought the old wood schoolhouse, sold off some of the wood, and hired a contractor to build a seven- bedroom two-story house at the ranch with the leftover wood. Grandma designed the house, copying features from our Uvalde house. One of the rooms was intended for use by Grandma and Grandpa Park, who had become too old to stay alone. They stayed with us till they died in 1928. I was off at school or had graduated, so I did not have a dedicated room in that house while growing up.

When Papa worked his bees, it was a big thing to be allowed to turn the large extractor barrel that whirled the honey away from the combs. He'd cut the combs into little squares, put them in 5 lb. cans, and then fill them with honey. During the WW2 years sugar was rationed. People used honey as their sweetener.

The ranch Charley began did so well that by 1913 the family purchased a Chevrolet touring car, one of the early automobiles in Zavala County. They used it to take their first vacation, a drive to see the new Medina Dam and Lake northwest of San Antonio. By 1915, Charley either bought or leased enough land to feed more and more cattle for sale to Pershing's soldiers along the border. By 1918 he was ranching 20,000 acres.

Toward the end of the First World War, the cattle market collapsed and Charley was forced to give up part of the leased land and to sell off what cattle he could. Hard times came and went for the ranching business for the next few years; still Charley was able to afford to send all his children to college.

The big ranch house served five generations of his family. Rarely were the two at home without some member of family around.

As he and Cecil aged, they relied more and more on family or hired help to run the ranch and they cut down operations to beekeeping and maintaining a herd of fifty cows with two bulls; selling off the calf crop each year. Still, one or more hogs were butchered each year so the family could share the lye soap, bacon, ham and chitlins. Charley maintained a year-round smokehouse for ham, beef and venison (in season). Cecil maintained her chicken flock with steady crop of fryers and layers. She gardened into her 90's, relying on hired help for the plowing. She continued to drive the family Chevrolet to town for the mail daily. They never owned anything but a Chevy.

Browns 1950 Chevrolet

Grandma's 1950 Chevrolet (Photo courtesy of Les Shaw.)

Stories of Mary Blanche Brown
as told to Shirley Wright

My questions and comments in italics

September 14-18, 1989

I was going to ask you. When you went to school, you're eight and Les is what? Six?

Six. Yes.

And was it like a one-room schoolhouse with all grades together or...

Oh, no. It had each room had, two grades. It was a ten-year school through high school. It's the one we live in now. It's our ranch house, you know. It was a big square and had two stories. The school, now our house, in Batesville was, we'll say up in here somewhere...at the end of that street. You know which street I'm talking about?

No.

You know—like you're coming to Dilley from Batesville—you know that road that goes to Uvalde. And that you're coming from the ranch here, and you're going towards La Pryor there. Here's the road that goes by the school. The school's right here. All right. Well, our house was at the end of this street. Very nice home there. An irrigation ditch was here. And this was the road to La Pryor. I'm not doing a very good job. This house was just like our house. They were twins. They were built by Bettie Belle's uncles.

Where's the post office?

The post office is down here somewhere.

Okay.

I'll show you where it is some day. I'll make that clearer later. But right now, I'll tell you the shape of the schoolhouse. It was a big square; two-story building and it had entrances on four sides. You've seen a picture of the school children lined up. And, it had a hall going through it, a big wide hall. Our first room was in here. They had two grades in there. They were big rooms. I can't remember now, but I'd say 30' x 30', maybe even bigger. And this grade, when they got here, they had three grades in a room. They had first and second here, and here they had third, fourth and fifth, and maybe even sixth. I don't know how the rest of it went, but it went up to the tenth grade. Two more rooms here. Then the upstairs was an auditorium with a stage. All of it was one great big auditorium—very big. Our first classroom was in here. There were twenty-six or eight children in the first grade. And, our house was up here. We had to cut across a field to save time. We crossed oat patches, two of them, crawled through a barbed wire fence, and we were there. Or, we walked down in front of where Bettie Belle's Grandma lived, which was down this way. But, we always crossed the fields. When they first put us in school, Mamma left us. She took us upstairs, and let us look out the window so we could see where our house was.

Oh, is that right?

And, we let her go then. But, we were scared to death. We were mortally afraid. And the older kids thought we were such curiosities that they would corral us...hold us right in here and say, We'll let you go if you'll talk Spanish"...they said, "talk Mexican." So we'd rattle something in Mexican, and they'd let us go. That's how...we were such oddities... so ranchero as the Mexicans would say. Oh, we were country. Scared of everybody. We only knew one person in school, and he was... you know... back to the ranch now...up across the highway, you know, was this land up here that Papa at one time owned. Although, Mamma said we didn't own it because we didn't pay for it all. I guess that's why she was mad and said we never owned it. But, to us, we owned it. And it was in our name for all our lifetime nearly, in those days. Well, anyway, Papa and Mr. Childress owned it together as partners. So Mr. Childress had the telephone business, and that's how come we get the first telephone. That's the first time I ever remember Mr. Childress's son came with him. Put our phone in the old house. Our phone was installed right there, right by the dining room table. First phone I ever saw—that I remember seeing. And he brought W. T. with him. That's how I knew W. T.

And he was the one child that you knew when you went to school?

That was it. W. T. Childress. And we stayed in Batesville School until 6th grade. When we finished 6th grade there, you were supposed to go to the high school, but we moved to Uvalde so that we'll have graduated from an accredited high school. So, Papa bought a house up there, and we all moved up. And, Papa came on weekends to visit us all those years. He always stayed at the ranch, he and his men that worked for him. And, we would go down there in the summer and stay the whole summer. But, we lived in Uvalde my four years, and then through Paul... when Paul finished. In Paul's last year in high school, he had to commute from Batesville to go to Uvalde School. He drove back and forth.

Now this house was on the ranch property, and the school you went to was in the town of Batesville?

Yes. It was in the town of Batesville. And we had a house in Batesville.

Okay, and you moved there when you were eight?

We moved over there when I was eight. Yes. Lived there till I was thirteen, and then we moved to Uvalde so I could go...so Leslie and I could enter high school. But, when we got up there we were amazed to learn that they had seven grades in the elementary, so they put us in the seventh grade because we had finished sixth. And, then, after one month, they decided to separate us because the work was so easy for me. See, I'm two years older... eighteen months older than Brother. And, the day they told me they were going to take me away, I'll never forget the face he made. I looked at that poor little face. And, he was just lost. I had him so under my thumb that he wouldn't answer a question unless I'd turn around and nod to him. He'd raise his hand then. That's how bossy I was over him, you know. I'd protected him all his days, and bossed him around... I know unmercifully as I look back. But, I'd hear his lessons. I'd see... I'd check his schoolwork... give him his spelling lesson. I'd correct his papers. I was his teacher in the evening. We were so close. And, I imagine the teachers saw that and knew that I ought to move away from him because he was too under me. Of course, I didn't know at the time, and I was scared to leave him. I felt terribly obligated. And, when I walked out of the room to go to high school that sad expression on his face tore my heart out. But, he got along just fine. He never had any trouble at all. He didn't set the world on fire, but he got along without me.

Now, how far behind you was he then?

One grade, so that made him graduate a year behind me. See, in other words, I skipped the seventh grade. I never had United States history. I missed that then. But, I never missed the rest of it. I don't know why. U. S. history was the only subject I missed that I know of, and I got along just fine. In fact, we got along pretty well because we were pretty fluent in Mexican... Spanish. That's how come in high school I took four years of Spanish. And, I took Latin one year, for the lack of something else to take, I took Latin. I had a pretty good high school record. We had a wonderful high school math teacher. Leslie was very good at math, and I was good at it. But, first thing you know, Leslie's taking roses to his teacher...Miss Burney. He loved Miss Burney. She was a geography teacher. He put roses under his cap. He didn't want us to know it, but he was taking teacher some flowers. He was so cute. I can see him now.

Brown children, Dandy is the pony

This would have been when he was in the sixth grade?

Yes. In August. From there on, you see, until I graduated. See I graduated in '24 and he graduated in '25. I remember the first Latin child that tried to go to high school in Uvalde. The older, some of the mean boys lit Roman candles and ran this child away from school. Can you imagine? I'll always remember that. I was horrified. The kid went home running with Roman candles being shot at his heels. Wasn't that cruel? How times, and we, have improved. We don't think anything, you know. They're our friends, of course. We're all the same blood now… the same image, and they think like we do. Things have changed considerably.

Now you said something once. I was curious if it was just an expression or if you really meant it, but you said the paisanos would whistle to come and play, and you'd go play with them. How did you play with a paisano?

That was fun. You'd chase them. You'd chase them and try to catch them, and they would act crippled or—like the doves—try to act crippled. Mislead you. I guess that's all we ever did was try to chase them and catch them. They were hard to catch. You couldn't...you'd have to have—let's see—later on there was a saying, see, we weren't supposed to kill paisanos because they killed rattlesnakes. So, they were our friends for that reason. But, I always thought they were telling me to come out and play. So, that's the way we did. We'd try to catch them. I don't say we caught them when we were little. But, when we got older...I remember, I started to tell this.

There was a saying that if you had boils—kids did have boils. If you'd kill a paisano and eat its meat, it would cure your boils. And, so, George Herman, who worked for Papa had boils, we all had boils. So, he killed a paisano, and they boiled the meat, and it did stop the boils. Whether it had anything to do with it; that was the saying. The meat tastes like chicken. I guess you could have eaten it. They were kind of bony, you know, stringy. But, I'm sure that the Mexican people probably ate them.

I'll tell you something else we always did that we learned from the Mexican children. You know this blooming dagger bush, the Spanish dagger that has those beautiful flowers in the middle?

Well it was the custom, we learned from the Mexican children to smother that in ashes and bake them, and they tasted so good. We'd eat the stalk.

What did it taste like?

About...tastes like asparagus.

Now, are you saying the stalk of the flower or?

I'm saying the flowers are on the stalk, and the stalk that they're on. Another thing that we did, we made tea out of cenizo leaves, and we also made tea out of pecan leaves for our playhouse.

Did you let them dry or?

No, no. We'd just boil them and drink them. And, that's fine tea. No telling what acids were in that pecan leaf... But, we drank it—no telling. But, there wasn't any leaf that I know of that we didn't try to experiment with. And, we ate berries that were in the woods, whatever we found. We ate lots of yellow berries, but especially we liked blueberries. They grow on some kind of tree-like thorny bush that had...we called them blueberries or blackberries. They're not the blueberry that you'd buy. We ate them, spitting out the seed. We ate mesquite beans galore. We just chewed on them like chewing gum...spit the seed out. In season, we made regular rounds to collect pitayas. They're just very good. They're akin to strawberry, I guess.

I don't know what that is.

You don't know what pitaya is? Have you not seen these beautiful purple blooms that are about as thick as my hand, and they have spine all over, spine, thorn all over them? They're green and they indent... have ridges. And they have the most beautiful blooming purple flower. They're cactus, and they are in bushes, and sometimes, they get as big as this table... the clump will be in the pasture. You don't see them so much anymore... simply died out. But, we knew where these were, and we made regular rounds. We'd go all around to all of our pitaya bushes, and go up across the highway and get on the other side in what we called the Childress... Brown/Childress...and go through those bushes. And I used to go there with Tony—even after I had Tony. I'd take him on my back, and I'd go pitaya hunting when I first had him. And, then, further back here was the sheep pen, where we loved to play with the sheep.

Now then, let me go from here...out this way to the garden. Now then, I would imagine the garden fence. Well, the way it is now, the garden fence is here. It's probably about like thus. And, in here was the sheep pen. And goat pen, later on, depending on whether we had sheep and goats. Now, back here are those old silos. And, way back here was the Mexican house. It was built of mesquite wood. Papa had the lumber cut by a sawmill on the Leona above the dam. Mesquite wood is very hard wood.

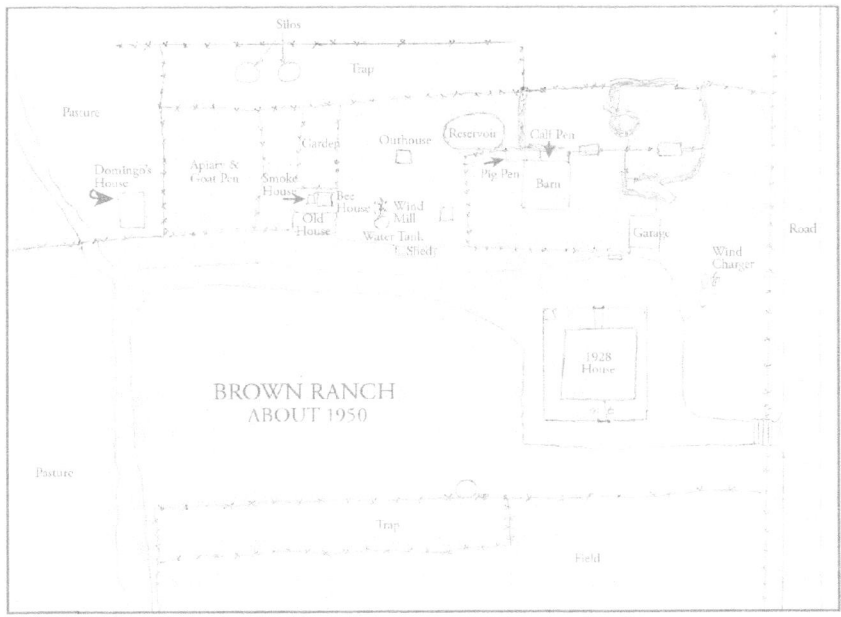

Brown Ranch about 1950

All right. Now, we had many happy hours riding the sheep or hitching up goats or something to little wagons and try to ride them, or go down there and just play for the heck of it.

When Papa finally abandoned this, the manure in here was about four or five feet tall, after they took the pen down around it. That's how many years that was there. And, what I started to tell now was the garden. Now, we had peach trees all in here and garden--at different times in a different place. But, a particular time, see down here was the bee house, now, let's see, to get back to this... now to go to the bee house, you just went down this way, see. But, my first memory was, that before it was the bee house. Gotta go back like that. There were two houses here. This was old Susie and Jose, and this was her daughter, Alcadia. And, her son was named Simon... the one we played with. There was an older brother, Pedro, I guess. Pedro was about 16 as I can remember him. He taught me my first Mexican words. Alcadia had a boy named Simon who is still living in Batesville and still thinks he's kin to us. He was Leslie's friend, Leslie's age.

33

But, Leslie and Simon and I played together when we were little. Old Jose was a blind man, but Susie helped Mamma in the house, and she spoke perfect English. I don't know where she learned it, but she helped Mamma when Hestel was born. She was the midwife for Mamma when Hestel was born, I remember. I guess that's a quick summary of it. And then I used to play...when they were digging these silos, after they finished that, Papa had them come up here and scrape out the reservoir. Papa had them come and make it deep. It's shaped oval you know. And we had this huge pecan tree here, and then the pens that are still there. But, I didn't tell where the toilet was. Of course, we always had to go to the outhouse. The outhouse was right back in here, too. When you came out of this house, you'd come back here. It was near the reservoir.

There were many stories, but they all had to do with when Papa and Mamma were taking their siesta. And, we never wanted to take a siesta, but our rule was you had to keep quiet and not wake them up. And, you had to lie there and be still. So, we got bolder and bolder, and we'd slip away from the front porch where we were supposed to be resting. Mostly it was so hot, they'd come out on the porch, too; but it depended on how many workmen were there, or if the workmen were not there. Be that as it may, the first disturber was the paisanos, who would come up on the porch, or they'd come on the front fence, and they'd go rrrrhh, rrrrhh, and to me that said, "Come out and play." And, so, we'd get out and play with them. And then, one thing led to another, and we loved mud pies, so we'd go up here to the reservoir dump because it had beautiful clay that came from the bottom of the silos, dredged from the silos, you see. We had all colors of clay, and we could make such lovely cups and saucers, make flowers and ornament them, you know, everything.

How old were you when all this was happening?

Oh, my first memories, you see: two and three, maybe three and four, right along in there. Leslie would tumble into the reservoir and we weren't—I had to be careful; so the first time he fell in, I pulled him back out, of course. Then maybe a bee would sting us on our big toes 'cause the bees were all getting water right there, too. It wasn't anything for a bee to sting him on his toes, and then we discovered sticking toes in the mud at the edge of the water was a mighty good feeling—relief. And, I found out going in to get him out of the mud was fun, when he slipped. And, first thing you know, we just made a habit of going in and taking a little rest in the reservoir. I remember Aunt Ada came up to see Mamma...or Mamma told me this...I don't know that I remember...and she was very frank. She said, "Charlie, Cecil, those kids are gonna drown in that reservoir." Anyway, she cautioned Papa and Mamma that we were gonna drown. But they had great faith in us. We survived. We didn't drown. We did learn to swim, but we didn't know we were swimming. We had no idea that we could swim. We did know that we didn't want the Mexican kids in there, and when we saw them, we resented their being there, although they were our only daily playmates.

Why didn't you want them there?

I don't know why...because in those days, that's how prejudiced Anglos were.

Anyway, we went on a trip to Grandma's, and we had to go in our surrey. It took all day to go to Dilley, and we stopped for our noon meal at a tank down in what is West country now, where the West ranch is. And, Mamma said, "Look". We saw this head sticking out of the water, coming across like a monster. Mamma said, "That's Papa." And we said, "Papa?" He'd gone on the far side of this lake and gotten in the water and was swimming over to us; just his head showing because he didn't have his clothes on. And she said, "He's swimmin'". We said, "swimmin'! That's swimmin'?" That's the first we ever knew anybody swimming. And, she said, "Yes, that's swimmin'". Here we'd been just about killing ourselves trying to walk on the surface of the water in our reservoir. And we could not stay up to walk on the surface of the water. But, we thought that was swimming because Mamma had a holy picture of our Lord walking on the water, and we'd been trying to do it. And, we never dreamed we were swimming until she said, "Look. That's Papa, he's swimmin'". That's the first time we ever saw anybody swimming.

That was kind of disappointing, wasn't it?

Yes. We said, "Good gracious, why we'd been swimming all the time." Here we were just knocking ourselves out to walk on the surface of the water. Now that's how country we were. We didn't see many people in those days. Few ever came to the ranch.

Now, I remember you telling the story about when the people would come...

Oh, my. When anybody'd come, which was very seldom—mostly it'd be cattle buyers. Well. Leslie would—after we got Hestel—Leslie would absolutely bring her and drag her under the bed. We'd grab our baby, and we'd take her and we'd crawl up under this bed.

Because the visitors said they were going to take her home with them.

They were gonna get our baby. Or, they're gonna get us, or something. They always had to notice us. We were very shy creatures. We really were. Very country.

And our daily lives were spent playing with the Mexican children. Always. They were our playmates, our friends, our only companions. They were older than we were. Most of them were older, but particularly the ones that dug the silo, because the mother was dead, and the big, older girl was a few years older than I am. She's old enough that she's supposed to cook for her father and her brothers and sisters. But, she loved to play, too. And so, our favorite game was to take our babies...we always took Hestel in the wagon. She'd take her baby in their wagon, and we'd go off in the woods and we'd play. And when things got boring, we'd play "battalia".

We'd say, "Let's battle. Combate."

She'd say, "Quiere combate?" And we'd play combate—means fight. And we'd fight with sticks...those big, long guajilla poles. And we'd fight each other, and when the game got too rough and we fell out...well, we had to flee for our lives. And, we'd come tearing home with our wagons and our babies and the hair flying, and we'd scrape under the fence as we crossed under the fence line, and the barbed wire would…well, we brought Hestel home all bloody one time…blood running right here, where she scraped on the barbed wires as we went under the fence. But, we got her home alive and the Mexican kids didn't kill us. And I imagine their babies got their heads bloody too, coming home. But, life was never dull.

Now, how old were you during this period?

This was from birth until we moved to Batesville to go to school, which was when I was eight.

You were eight?

When we moved to Batesville.

You were eight before you ever went to school?

Yes. I was eight years old when I started. See we had to wait. They wouldn't move to town, send me to school until Leslie was old enough to go too, because they didn't want to leave the ranch. So, I was older than he. And we were in the same grade. You see, that's what made me the bossy type, 'cause I bossed him all the time. See, Mamma told me now early on when Simon and Leslie and I would play together, one of our games was going around looking at the bird's nests, and looking at the eggs checking all the hatchlings, getting pitaya or maybe marking pear with a knife or stuff like that…or maybe just browsing around on the cow trails. But, Mamma said we shouldn't rob the birds' nests so I was always the cover, and Leslie and Simon got in the bird's nest. But, that was a no-no, and she would threaten their lives. They would say they didn't do it, and I'd tell Mamma and she'd believe me. So Leslie said. She always believed me. Anyway, he'd get a paddlin'. So that broke them of robbing birds' nests. Mamma wouldn't have that. But, we all could look, so we always looked.

I'll say my earliest memory is of living in the old ranch house. At that time, it was completely surrounded by mesquite. We had no fields in front of the house, and you couldn't see —there wasn't much of a road—there was just a wagon road up where the Pearsall highway is now. And, maybe, the only people we saw were, perhaps once a month, the Hart family who lived down below us, about ten miles down the Leona, would come to town. And, I remember, Grandfather Hart had been bitten by a rattlesnake, so he had an affliction—he was crippled a little bit. He would invariably stop and have a drink of water from the family dipper, you know, that hung on the porch, and talk a while. And frequently he'd take a meal with us.

But that's about the only people we ever saw, was old man Hart, and later on, his son, Jack Hart, who's the father of Jackie Hart that we all know. He was Leslie's age. But, anyway, Grandma Hart we never saw in those days till years later. But Grandpa Hart would go up to Batesville once a month to get his supplies.

I'll draw you a plan of the ranch house and the garden and the sheep pen and the two Mexican houses that were down south of us. Later on, one of these Mexican houses became Papa's bee house, and the other one was torn down. It was just a shanty. But, I loved to go down to the Mexican houses because that's where Susie and her husband, Jose, lived. And their daughter, Alcadia, lived in the other house with her sons—she had two sons— Pedro and Simon. Simon was a little younger than Leslie, and we played with Simon a lot.

But, our early days, we'd prowl around in the woods. The boys would look at bird's nests and see what kind of speckled eggs they had. And our Mother told us never to disturb a nest because the bird would abandon it—the eggs. Mamma cautioned me to be sure to report to her if Leslie and Simon disturbed the nest. That was a punishable offense. Also, it caused me to be called a tattletale by Leslie and Simon, but I did manage to bring them up right—to be upright citizens.

And, some of the things that we'd do to play would be maybe to go spend one whole day prowling in the woods, killing rats because there were many, many wood rats in the country, and you could always locate their den by seeing a big pile of sticks maybe three feet high with a lot of coverage over it. And the fun was to burn the wood part—set fire to it—and watch the snake or the rat or the rabbit or whatever was down there come out. And the object was to get the rat. And we'd have a dog with us, old Viejo was our dog. Incidentally, Viejo didn't die until he was 12 years old. Old Viejo would grab the rat if he could get him and if the rat could escape, he'd climb up a tree, and then we'd beat on the tree with a hoe, or shake the limb and try to make the rat fall out. Or if we could reach him we'd try to catch him by the tail and his tail skin would slick off and there'd be just that. But, invariably we got the rat because we made him come out of that tree some way, and the dog would then shake him to pieces. And lots of times we'd get a rattlesnake out of that den, too. We'd kill him with a hoe.

We were allowed to have a can of kerosene, a garden hoe, and the little red wagon to carry our supplies. And so we spent many hours prowling in the woods.

How old were you?

Well, this was between—before we were six—before we moved to Batesville I'm talking about. And, it was a…there were about three years there that the wood rats were just taking the country. They were really bad.

And, you never got bitten?

No, we never got bit by anything. Maybe a squirrel, a ground squirrel, bit us. We learned soon not to grab a ground squirrel by the back of the neck, had to be kind of careful. But, it didn't hurt.

Isn't it amazing that they would let you have kerosene and light fires! Would you have let your kids do that?

No. I'd have died. I'd have worried myself sick. But, don't you see, that must have given us lots of courage. We had responsibility.

Yes. It's just hard for me to think of little old Grandma allowing those things, you know.

But, we did. See, why she allowed it...because when she was a child that's how she played. They even bottled snakes in glass jars when Mamma was little. We never got that bold that we'd bottle snakes. And we'd just play around in the woods all day. We got a little bit older, and they let us cook out. We had a sack of brown flour—which we called Mexican flour because it was cheaper. And, we could have broken dishes. We'd pack an old iron stove lid—that was our grill. Then our cups were canned milk cans that you burned the ends off of. And we could have molasses in our camp house—canned molasses. And, with flour, then we could make our own bread, you see. And we'd cook pinto beans, that kind of stuff. So we loved to cook out. We always had fried potatoes. Yeah, we were allowed to do all those things. Another thing we used to do, we'd take our wagon, our kids and our friends, can of kerosene oil and take a hoe and we'd go back where the old—you know where that reservoir is, back of the ranch house down there, away from the house—well, out in that territory, there were lots of big, tall mesquite trees with lots and lots of rat's nests. It was legitimate to burn a rat's nest and when you'd burn a rat's nest, first might come out a rabbit, and then might come out a rattlesnake, and certainly might come out the rat. And when he'd come out, he'd go up the nearest tree, and there we'd be pulling, trying to catch him. Finally, we'd get him by the tail—his tail would skim off—and we'd hack at the burning fire to get the snake, if we could kill him like that. 'Course we started the fire on the rat's nest—just a big pile of wood, see, over the hole, and we'd start it with our kerosene oil.

Brown family in Uvalde

Speaking about the family picture made when we lived in Uvalde after the flu season. We were scared to death, but they'd bundle us all up to have our pictures made. Talk about scared, sober sides...look at us. Look at Norma—belligerent type.

After you had the flu?.

We were living in Uvalde then, had to be within, I'd say before, let's see, I'd say about 1925. Let's see...1925, maybe. No, I graduated in '24 so it's before that. Let's make it '22, somewhere in there. How old do you think I am? That's the way I wore my hair—rolled behind. Paul doesn't look very old. Norma looks like she's 8, and I'm 8 years older than she is. Do I look 16? Let me see, might be 15 there. All right, suppose I'm 15 so that would be...I was born in '07 and add eight. That would be 22. Uh huh, that'd be about right.

What else will I tell you about?

What kind of dog was Viejo?

Oh, he was just an old yellow mutt. I don't know as he was anything —he was a mongrel. He was a hound dog, let's put it that way. At least he had big, flappy ears. He didn't particularly go for children, as we know dogs now. You had to stay away from him. In fact, I carry a scar to this day where he bit me when I went out to share his supper with him one night. In those days, you fed your dog table scraps. Mamma had fed the table scraps in a little old enamel plate that had been my baby plate, and I saw it out in the yard, and the dog was eating out of it. And, I went up—I was very small—but I do remember being bit. And, he got me right here, and I have a scar right there where the light scar is. But, Mamma plastered me back together with the membrane of an egg. See, that was what we used for adhesive tape, was the membrane of an egg yolk. It grew together—just had a very small scar, but, I never tried to eat with Viejo again. I learned that it wasn't profitable.

Another thing I remember, we had some stumps in the front yard that had to be burned out. I guess we had trees there. And, the glow of the coals was just perfectly beautiful—a pink glow with ashes over it, you know. And Mama stuck her head out the window and said, "Young lady. Whatever you do, don't you dare put your foot in that—where those ashes are! Don't you dare!" Well, I couldn't wait to walk on those ashes. So, I did. I'll have you know, I walked in those ashes. And, of course, right under those ashes was live coals. So I did get my bare feet burned. And then I had to sit for a day or two with my feet in a pan of soda water. Mamma put soda, baking soda in the water. And that's the way I soaked my feet. But, I did learn a lesson. But if she hadn't told me" don't you dare—young lady, don't you dare step," I wouldn't have thought about it. I would have known better. But, I did.

And let's see what else I recall. I recall once going down toward the sheep pen in my bare feet stepping on a little baby rattler head, but I jumped so high he didn't get me. And, I can still feel that head though on my bare heel. The way I felt it, I really leapt.

What else we did? We tried to ride the goats and sheep. We'd take our wagon down and try to make harness for it. Try to hitch up a goat to pull the wagon. Invariably the goats would go wild or the sheep would go wild and scrape us off on the fence. See, this was a wooden pen and the logs would really tear you up, so we got our knees skinned and everything.

I remember once when they were working cattle, and there was a mad cow in the barnyard. And it had been our habit to go climb up on the barn and watch the cow work. We could see them dipping' the cattle or whatever they were doing. Paul was just a baby then, and I saw Paul wander up there into that barnyard where that mad cow was. And I saw the mad cow challenge—threaten to butt him, and I knew he was a goner. He was just a tiny little fellow. And about that time here came Willie Ponds, a boy who worked for my daddy, riding horseback. He's coming from town to work for the day, and he saw what was happening. The old cow had Paul down and was butting him, and Willie galloped down from where the Batesville road is now. He galloped down and jumped the fence and saved the boy's life. Picked him up—the cow had slobbered all over him. Mamma cleaned Paul up. And we'd been up on the barn roof so many times tormenting that old cow. We used to slide on the tin roof of that barn—pull our toenails off on the brads and all of that. But there was always something to do around there.

Papa put in a sheep vat—dipping vat for sheep. And it was really, to us, a concrete bathtub. We had a big rain, so we thought, "Oh, great". So we just, while they weren't around, we just went up and took a bath in that—with the sheep dip in it. And later on, we did the same thing—we had a big rain, and we had the dipping vat for the cattle. Came a big rain and just filled that dipping vat up full, so we all put on our bathing suits and went up there and swam across there. You know, one end you could slide in. Well, we never had such fun in our lives, but I guess that really toughened our skin. There wasn't anything that we didn't explore or know about that was going on around our ranch.

Blanche Brown Wright, Teacher

Transcribed by Shirley Wright

Blanche taught school for 51 years in the State of Texas. She and her daughter-in-law, Shirley, compiled her memories:

The Brown family moved to Batesville, in order that my Brother Les and I attend school.

Somehow, we adjusted to school-life, our fine first-grade teacher, and our classmates. We soon had a well-worn path through an oat field as a short cut between our house and school. We attended the Batesville School through the elementary grade, moving back to the ranch to spend our summers. My father eventually bought us a little rubber-tired buggy and a Shetland pony in order that we children might drive out to the ranch after school on school days.

We were two very shy, scared, country children our first day of school. Some older children corralled us and would not let us go until we 'talked Mexican'.

Since we were in the same class, it was my habit to see that Leslie did his homework and studied. Leslie would recite only when I would nod to him to volunteer an answer that I knew he could give. How embarrassed I was once when he volunteered and spelled "BisKit" (biscuit)!

After the first six grades we moved to Uvalde to enter high school—only to learn Uvalde had a 7th grade before high school. After a month in the

7th grade, I was taken out of the 7th grade leaving my dear little brother. He looked so distressed, but evidently the separation was for the best. He did very well without me to boss him.

Our wonderful second-grade teacher is the one who first inspired me to want to become a teacher. Her influence was so great that, even out of her jurisdiction, we children tried to do the right thing all the time. We would have felt obligated to tell this beloved teacher about any fights, etc., we had at home. Our wrong doings pained her deeply, or so we thought.

She read "Uncle Remus" stories on Fridays. She regaled us with stories of the Blue Ridge Mountains of Virginia, where she had lived as a child. She made daily inspection and kept records with columns headed "Brushed My Teeth Daily", "Hands Clean", "Nails Cleaned" etc.

Also, she had a map of Texas on which to record the names of those who knew their lessons. Any indication that one had not been studying, and he would find himself no longer a Texan. If one later redeemed himself he could become a resident of a bordering area. He could not get back into Texas until the next time report cards were distributed. Also, we had competition on various subjects. Furthermore a "memory gem" daily, was our answer to roll call. It was unthinkable to go to school unprepared. I give Mrs. Wilson credit for any degree of photographic memory I may have developed.

That year I persuaded my father to paint blackboards on the walls of our hayloft and to bring in from the ranch a number of bee boxes to serve as desks. I persuaded the weaker classmates to attend my Saturday School. Everyone who came improved in arithmetic and spelling, their play-teacher's favorite subjects at the time. This play school was held for several years. I was never without pupils—there were my younger brothers and sisters in the event no one else came. A side effect was that I participated in Interscholastic League spelling and was the county champion all the way through the high-school years.

When my brother and I reached the seventh grade level, the family moved to Uvalde, Texas in order that we might have the advantage of the excellent accredited high school in Uvalde. My first impression of Uvalde High School was one of disappointment—girls had to play softball! (I had excelled in hardball style up until that time.) After the first month in the seventh grade I was separated from my brother and moved into the freshmen class in high school. I really did not think my brother capable of doing schoolwork without me. It had reached the point that if the teacher asked a question that I knew my brother could answer, I would signal him to raise his hand to recite! We survived.

Uvalde is a beautiful town with its large oak and pecan trees and flowers. We had two interesting routes to school. The one that led through an abandoned cemetery with its interesting markers also took us by the home of Mr. John Nance Garner, even then a famous citizen. The other, and longer, route also had merit, since it passed directly by a bakery. After school, there had private piano lessons at the Convent, which was not far from high school. I might have been more successful as a pianist had it not been for the fact that the teacher required me to stay an extra hour to accompany my brother who was learning to play "Old Black Joe", on the violin.

The Uvalde teachers were among the very best! No finer teachers exist than our teachers of mathematics and Spanish. Our teacher of Latin later became a state superintendent. The four years soon ended. I graduated from this accredited high school in May, and in June 1924, entered the University of Texas. I wanted to prepare to teach as soon as possible.

Winning first place in free-style swimming in girls' physical education was probably my most self-satisfying accomplishment my freshman year. Also, I made third base in girls' baseball (hardball). I had Miss Anna Hiss and met Dr. Annie Webb Blanton. Both Dr. I. T. Nelson and Dr. O.B. Douglas, who in later years sponsored my thesis, were among my teachers during my undergraduate years. Little did I dream that the football hero who was a classmate in Miss Lilia M. Casis' advanced Spanish grammar class would someday play an important part in my life. Mr. J. W. Nixon came to Laredo in 1929 first as supervisor of physical education. He then became principal of the junior high, then of the senior high school, and until August 31, 1973 was the Superintendent of Laredo Public Schools.

I stayed out of school my third college year to teach. (My father had three children in college at the same time—in those days there were no federal funds, etc., to help college students.) I signed up for a correspondence course before I left the University. My first school was really in an isolated region—about equidistant from Eagle Pass, Carrizo Springs and Crystal City, Texas. I boarded in the home of a former member of the Texas House of Representatives.

My First School

Upon completion of 90 hours of college work in 1926, I was granted a certificate to teach either in high school or in grade school.

I was overjoyed when I was offered a school in Cometa, Texas. This was called a Common School District. Zavala County did not have a school superintendent, but County Judge Hunt served in this capacity, along with his other duties. Of course the fact that Mrs. Erskine was a childhood friend of my mother's in Frio County must have had something to do with my getting the position.

It was established that my salary was to be $75 per month for the seven-month school term. I was to live with Mr. & Mrs. Frank Harris. Mrs. Harris was one of the school trustees. Her husband had recently retired from the Texas Legislature. Their daughter, Lutilla, lived in Carrizo Springs with an older sister, Mrs. Mary White, in order to attend Carrizo Springs High School.

The Cometa School building was located on the Crystal City-Eagle Pass road. It was truly a house by the side of the road—there was little traffic in 1926-1927. I thought of it as being 18 miles to Carrizo Springs, 14 miles to Crystal City, and 30 miles to Eagle Pass.

Just walking from the Harris place to school took courage. As I recall, it seems that the Harris farm was located at least two miles from the schoolhouse. I didn't dread the long walk through a pasture until I learned that a huge Brahma bull patrolled the area. And, he was no respecter of fences. Needless to say I discovered a longer, safer route by following a dry creek bed and climbing through several barbed wire fences. For a while I thought this route was haunted. Every day as I passed under a bridge, I'd hear a hideous hiss. I finally discovered the source—an owl perched on a banister of the bridge! There was an ancient cemetery in the woods, but because of that old Toro I never got to explore.

After reaching the safety of the road, I'd walk by Mr. & Mrs. Erskine's house. From there I'd have little Mary Jane who was my star pupil. We'd walk up the hill, pass by and greet her Grandmother Erskine, and one of Mary Jane's uncles. They lived in a two-story house not too far from the Cometa school. I think the Harris place was about two miles from the school; at least it seemed that it was.

The school was a large, one-room, rectangular-shaped, wooden building, well lighted by many large windows, and freshly painted white. There was a cast iron wood-burner heater, which was set on a tin mat, a wooden teacher's desk that was mounted on a raised platform, and many wooden desks for students. Judging from the many student desks found in the room, the school enrollment in earlier years must have been much greater. That year I think something like fourteen pupils were expected to attend school, however, possibly the greatest number in attendance any one day would not have averaged five. I recall several children whose surname was English, but my most faithful pupil was Mary Jane. That was her first year of school. She received so much individual attention that she did all the work of a first and then a second grader.

Occasionally, my star pupil would develop a toothache. If oil of cloves didn't work, I'd walk her home. But pupils or no pupils, I sat in the building until 4:00 PM. I wanted to earn my pay. On days when I was there alone, I gathered mesquite gum and boiled it in water to make glue. Then, using some of the broken window panes I found under the building as my canvas, I'd paint a design in glue, then sprinkle the many different shades of red and brown clay and, for green, mesquite leaves that were in the school yard to make a picture. At least the time passed pleasantly.

Once a month, my father would come, on a Friday after 4:00 PM, and take me to Uvalde to visit my family over the weekend. I recall the unpaved, zigzagged road that skirted the many sections of land along the way. There were many gates and too many wire gaps one had to stop and open. On one occasion, after a big rain, the trip back to Cometa, from Uvalde, took seven hours. We were in a Model T Ford pickup.

I realize now what a sacrifice it was for my father, Mr. Charles Brown, to make that long drive from our ranch, which is east of Batesville. He always spent the weekends with the family in town in the years we lived there in order for the children to attend school.

Events in the Harris home that I recall: When son, Frank, was planting and irrigating, he'd pump water from a deep well in order to fill a reservoir. This water was warm enough for me to take a swim, even in cold weather. A bath otherwise meant a washtub by the kitchen stove. The farm, where I lived, had a telephone, a party line with 14 families connected. Mr. Harris used to tease me by ringing his own number, then waiting a few minutes, until he'd hear several telephone receivers being lifted. The he'd say, "That's all, ladies." It was his idea that everybody eavesdropped—especially on a very young schoolteacher.

And that was the year we all went to Eagle Pass one day to attend the marriage of son, Frank Harris, to Miss Rosita Delamaine. The wedding took place in the Episcopal Church.

The school building served the community as a meeting place. I recall attending several dances. The dances were attended by entire family groups and were well chaperoned. Mr. Harris was rather strict about dance partners for Lutilla and me. Occasionally, we were invited out on a Friday night to attend a picture show, either in Crystal City or in Carrizo Springs.

All too soon the school year ended. With the money I'd saved, I went back to Texas University and completed my degree. I told a university friend about Cometa and the school year 1927-28 was in the capable hands of Rose Brodovsky. She loved teaching at Cometa.

As a postscript, I might add that when I retired from the Laredo Public Schools in 1979 after 51 years of teaching, an honored guest was my very first and star pupil, Mary Jane Erskine Laird.

Important to me was that I was made a member of Sigma Delta Pi, national honorary society for Spanish majors. I had done my practice teaching in Spanish and had earned a Life Teaching Certificate when I graduated June 1928.

Rosenberg School

My first teaching position after graduation from college was in Cottonwood School, Rosenberg, Texas. The position was obtained through a cattle-buyer who came to our ranch that summer. He just happened to be a school trustee, also. I taught all the high school subjects and was also the principal, because of the B.A. Degree. Radios were the "in" thing that year. Our county superintendent expected to unify instruction throughout the county. She expected to broadcast lectures and give tests to all the schools via radio. It was my duty to have our students hear these radio offerings, but all I could get was static. At the end of the school year, I decided not to re-apply. Transportation was a great problem. The two-mile walk and the terrific mud were too much. Being from the arid southwest, I was unaccustomed to so much rain!

That summer, I attended Draughons' Business College, taking a combined business course and Spanish. Before the summer was over, I was offered a position as bookkeeper by a San Antonio firm, which had a branch-office in Laredo, Texas. Although, I had never been to Laredo, I accepted the offer. By the time the school year was about to begin, I decided I could do the bookkeeping after school and Saturdays. I applied for a teaching position and was placed as teacher of 3rd grade in the Heights School.

The following year, I was transferred to the just-completed L. J. Christen Junior High, where I taught arithmetic. I continued the bookkeeping on the side. In 1931, I decided to go back home to live with my parents on the ranch and to teach in the Batesville High School. There, I taught Spanish, mathematics and business courses. Also I coached girls' volleyball and tennis—the girls' doubles went to State for their tennis ability that year— through their own ability—not as a result of tennis instruction from me.

Edward Wright

On Thanksgiving Day, 1931, I married Edward V. Wright, a native Laredoan. The following summer, I moved back to Laredo, this time to reside permanently. As our first child was expected in February 1933, I did not teach the school year 1932-1933.

In the spring of 1933 I accepted a job as time-payment clerk with a mail order firm here in Laredo. Starting the following September and for six years I taught sub-first grade at Nye Elementary School (Webb County). Also, I continued to work as part-time time-payment clerk the next three years. After the six-year span in which I taught at Nye, I returned to L. J. Christen School and the teaching of arithmetic in junior high. By this time our family had increased to four children, Edward Jr., Mary Paul, and Pat and Mike (twins).

In January of 1942 I was transferred to Martin High School, where I have remained. Mr. J. W. Nixon had been made principal of Martin High the summer of 1941. He had been my principal at Christen School. It was his confidence in me, as a mathematics teacher, that made me resolve to study to become as efficient a mathematics teacher as time, family, and finances permitted.

In 1938 (summer) my parents kept my small children in order that I attend the University of Texas to begin work towards my Master's Degree. One of my most enjoyable courses that summer was "Life and Literature of the Great Southwest" taught by J. Frank Dobie. He especially liked a term paper I wrote on the "Paisano" and summoned me to his office to ask me to consider majoring in English. I decided to continue as planned. I took my Master's Degree in August, 1949, with a major in Educational Psychology and a split minor—English and Spanish. My thesis was entitled "An Analysis of Word Problems in Elementary Algebra".

By the time I had acquired my Master's Degree, it was about time to start our children's college educations. Since 1949, I have spent many hours taking correspondence courses, field courses, night courses at Laredo Junior College, plus two summers (21 semester hours of mathematics, graduate level) at Fort Hays Kansas State College—building up a major in mathematics. Also, I have taken periodic Federal Entrance Exams in order to familiarize myself with the type of problems asked on Civil Service examinations. A side result was that I have had offers of government jobs, but would never willingly give up my teaching career. One fall semester, I was able to go on Saturdays to Corpus Christi, Texas, to study a modern mathematics course offered through the auspices of the Texas Education Agency.

Through the years, since the Laredo Junior College opened its doors, I have been an occasional part-time teacher in their evening program—generally teaching first year algebra or business mathematics. Last spring, I taught trigonometry; this past summer I taught a mathematics course for nurses. Also, besides my duties at Martin High, as a mathematics teacher, for years I have been a member of the Scholarship Committee and a senior sponsor. When a mathematics study center first opened in February of 1965, one teacher was assigned to help the students after school with their mathematics. Attendance soon increased until three mathematics teachers plus two student-assistants were required. I taught in the remedial mathematics program approximately four years—at first we donated our services; later, we were remunerated by some federal program. This was followed by a two-year period during, which we worked for the pleasure of seeing students improve in mathematics. I have taught mathematics in regular summer school many times; also I have taught several summers under the Federal Enrichment Program.

In addition to my regular duties as teacher of mathematics, for a period of eight years, I was the sponsor of the Courtesy Service Club, the honor service organization for girls at Martin High School. Membership in this club is by nomination from the faculty followed by balloting by both faculty and girls who are already members. To be a member, a girl must have perfect conduct grades and very good grades in all her subjects. This fine group of girls renders many hours of unselfish service to the school and to the community. They help with registration, usher at all locally held Martin High football games. Each year they help with registration and selling of programs when the Border Olympics are held, generally in March. They check tickets and usher at all Civic Music Programs. If a teacher's convention is held in Laredo, they are there to help. It was a privilege to work with the Courtesy Service Club, although it required many extra hours of my time. I had to give up the club when my husband had his first heart attack.

Mary Paul, our daughter, is a graduate of the University of Texas prepared to be a teacher. The three sons are graduates of Texas A&M University. Edward Jr. is an electrical engineer and the twins are civil engineers. My husband died in 1961, shortly after attending the twin's graduation exercises at Texas A&M. The children are now all married and no longer live in Laredo. There are fifteen grandchildren. My students at Martin High are my other children. The teaching of mathematics to these wonderful young friends makes life very pleasant and very rewarding.

To keep mentally alert and refreshed, after teaching the long term and sometimes the summer term, I generally take a trip or go camping. I especially enjoy swimming, fishing, sewing and the reading of mystery stories. I like to keep abreast of world affairs, and to learn all I can about other places, people, their customs and history. My travels have taken me through most of the United States and Mexico. In the summer of 1964, I spent six weeks in Europe, touring the continent, England, Ireland, and Scotland.

In the summer of 1971, and again in the summer of 1972, I went on thirty-five-day tours of the Orient. My travels took me to Japan, Taiwan, Thailand, Singapore, Malaysia, the Philippines, Hong Kong, Okinawa, and Hawaii. An effort was made to learn something about geography, climate, government, history, and education in each place visited.

Like most teachers, when school starts again, I am glad. Each year it is my hope that I can do a better job of teaching. If I had any degree of success in teaching it is due in great part to my having had wonderful parents, an understanding husband, very inspiring teachers, and very encouraging administrators, who let me know they have confidence in me.

My Autobiography

Blanche's high school English theme

Although I am a noted writer, and often called upon to write, I have never been called upon to write on such an interesting subject as "My Autobiography". Some people are called vain, because they write their autobiographies; therefore, I want it to be known that I am not writing this because I am egotistical, but because the teacher is inquisitive.

I have been told that an autobiography must contain nothing but the truth. For this reason I shall try to be careful. Probably in later years children will take my autobiography for a model, and I do not want them to prevaricate.

It was a difficult matter to trace the homes and names of my ancestors. I have heard of people that can be hired to trace ancestors, but I was afraid they might go too far. I have heard so much about evolution.

Mother's father came from Scotland, and grandmother came from Kentucky. She was of Irish descent. My grandmother's mother had never done a bit of work in her life, until she came to Texas. Her hands were plump and white because the slaves had always done everything for her. When my grandmother was fifteen years old, she went with her parents, back to Kentucky. The old slaves were still around the old plantation. Grandmother says that they all rushed in to see 'Miss Mahalia', and that all the old Negresses exclaimed, "Oh! Look at poor Miss Mahalia's pretty hands. Chile, we might have known that you would go off down to Texas and ruin them."

These great-grandparents had to leave their plantation because they could not run it. Lincoln had freed their slaves. Great-grandfather taught music in conservatory in Philadelphia before he met 'Miss Mahalia' and came to Texas. My father's parents came from Missouri, and they too, were of Irish descent. I have not fully decided what my father himself is. Mother says that he is a Bohemian, but I believe that he denies the charge.

I was born February 7, 1907. I lived on the ranch until I was seven years old. They say that I was pretty when I was little, and I am sure I must have been because I have often heard the saying, "pretty children are ugly grown people".

Some Mexican children lived on the ranch. They used to come to the fence to admire me and my brother. I used to wait for them and trade slices of bread for their tortillas. I thought I was profiteering, and I suppose they thought the same thing. During this stage of ignorance I heard grown people talking about the revolutions in Mexico. I heard them talking about American people moving to town because of their fear of Mexicans. As we lived on a public road I thought I had better take it upon myself to insure our safety; consequently, I just called on the Mexican children and asked them about it. I was certain that they would know. As I remember, they did not know, but they promised to save me in case of any danger.

My father had some underground silos dug near the house. After they had been dug about thirty feet deep, water was struck. When I saw the water running in, I was greatly frightened because I was sure the water would fill the silos and drown everyone.

I saw the first eclipse that I can remember of, when I was in the first grade. The larger girls told me the world was coming to an end. They nearly scared me to death. I cried and refused to believe the teacher when she told me better. I was really frightened when I saw my first aeroplane. I was outside and saw it fly over the house. My brother came running around the house and exclaimed, "Mother, oh! Mother, was that God?" I knew what it was; but nevertheless, I was so scared that I trembled. I saw my first train when I was staying at my grandmother's. There were some freight cars on the railway track. Grandmother wanted me to cross the track and go across the street to a hotel. Like most grandmothers, she finally consented not to send me.

The greatest horror of my life was the thought of Mother and Dad's leaving me. It used to seem to me that in every crowd people were trying to steal me by pushing me away from Mother. Just as sure as I ever went to a picnic or barbecue, I invariably got lost. Then I would cry until someone would come and ask me whose little girl I was. I never liked to be called a little girl either. If they took me back to Mother, she always scolded me for running off.

Christmas always appealed to me as one of the happiest occasions in my life. The only idea that I do not like is that idea of having Christmas just once a year. I could never remember from one Christmas to the next.

When I was seven years old, we moved to town. Mother was to start us in school. I never felt so important in my life as I did the first day I went to school, but I was so frightened that I kept my pride to myself. My brother and I were taken to school and left in care of the teacher; but before Mother left us she took us to a window and showed us our home just across the way. Here she left us standing. The teacher finally persuaded us to leave the window, but before I did, I shut my eyes and turned my head away from home. I felt that that would probably be my last vision of home.

When I was thirteen years old we moved that we might graduate from an accredited school. I was heartbroken when I was put into the seventh grade. I had wanted to be a freshman so that the boys at home might not finish school before I did. After a month of seventh grade work, they put me into the freshman class. I actually began to believe that dreams did come true a few times. When I was taken into the freshman class they were reciting "General Science". I had never had any branch of science. I thought the pupils the smartest I had ever seen in my life. I came home and told Mother that they even knew what made bread rise.

I suppose I took other subjects when I was a sophomore, but I distinctly remember one, Biology. I thought Mr. Henderson was the easiest teacher I had ever seen. I can remember once that he asked me if I had my notebook ready. I told him yes, and he replied that he would give me "A". He did not even look at the notebook. As a junior, I think that my mind was on "geometry" most of the time. I had been informed beforehand that no one could ever pass in geometry the first time he took it. Miss Anthon was not half as bad as I had imagined she was. At first, I was afraid to do anything.

Ever since I was a child, I have said that I wanted to be a schoolteacher. I wanted to teach and get even with the children for what teachers have done to me. I have since decided that this would be cruel because these children would be perfectly innocent. I once read of a little girl that could not draw a picture of her highest ambition. Other members of the class drew soldiers, sailors, pretty ladies, etc. The teacher asked the little what her ambition was, and if she could not draw it, that she might tell what it was.

"Oh!" said the little girl, "I want to be married." No wonder, it is that she could not draw her highest ambition. She would never draw anything (money) from it in later years. At present my ambition is to get a good grade in Chemistry and to graduate.

My Autobiography

Leslie Brown

English 4 B

February 2, 1925

There are two reasons for my writing an autobiography. The first and main reason is that our teacher requires us to, and the other is that I think it is an interesting topic to write about. I was never very fond of writing themes; although this seems to be something like a theme I think it will be much easier, or at least much more interesting, and I am going to do my best.

I know very little about my ancestors any farther back than my grandfathers and grandmothers because, I suppose, I have never tried to find out anything. My grandfather, on my father's side died when I was very small, therefore I know nothing about him save that which has been told me. He had a large ranch and farm together and on these he and my grandmother lived. To them were born seven children all of whom are still living. My grandfather on my mother's side came from Scotland when a very little baby. His father died on the ship on the way over and his mother died soon after the landed. He had a brother and three sisters older that himself. They were strangers in the new country and there were very few people living at the place they landed. Since he and his brother and sisters were too small to make their own living they had to be taken care of so one family adopted him and his brother and another family adopted his three sisters. It was not very long before the family that adopted his sisters moved away. He has never seen or heard of them since. He was also a ranchman.

I was born August 18, 1908 on my father's ranch near Batesville. My father usually kept a family of Mexicans on the ranch to help work it. Since we lived in the country the Mexican children were the only companions my older sister and I had most of the time. We built a playhouse in which we would usually cook and eat our own meals for we seldom ate a meal at home. Since we played with the Mexicans all the time we soon learned to talk Spanish almost as well as they. When our parents wanted to talk to a Mexican they would usually get one of us to act as interpreter for them. Our chief occupation then was hunting bird nests, rabbits, and rats. We did not have any work to do since we were only four or five years of age. We had a large number of bird's nests, which we visited every day to see if the eggs had hatched. I remember once we found a rabbit's nest in which there were small rabbits. The Mexican children got them out and said they were going to take them home, but we told them they were not. We quarreled with them a little, but it soon turned into a rock fight. Since we were out-numbered and were afraid they would make an escape with the rabbits, we made out as though we were just playing and told them to come we would all play with the rabbits a while. This they agreed to do. We talked friendly to them, and very soon we were good friends again. Just as soon as we got the rabbits we started home for we knew they would not follow us into the house. Our opponent tried to catch us, but we got the start of them, and as it was not very far to the house, we beat them there. In this way we got the rabbits for ourselves, but made the Mexican children our enemies again. Within two or three days, the rabbits died so we gave them back to the Mexican children and it was not long until we were friends again. Almost every day we would go on a rat chase. We would go to the rat's nests, set them on fire and as the rats came out we would kill them with sticks. Sometimes we would kill as many as twenty rats in a day in this manner. Many times we would go as far as a mile from home, but we did not get tired for we rode sticks for horses and we imagined we did not get tired then.

In 1914 our parents moved to Batesville so they could send us to school. One can imagine how we felt and acted since we had lived in the country all our lives and had never been in a group of strange people without the company of our parents before. We managed to make friends though very soon and after about two weeks we did not mind going to school, in fact we liked to go. All the time we went to school in Batesville there were never anymore than ten pupils in our class and not more than eighty in the whole school. Since there were so few pupils in the school almost all the boys played together. We played baseball, basketball, black man, marbles, and many other games. Sometimes the older boys played tennis and we pitched washers or played marbles. The school was so small it had not entered into the athletic league but twice before we moved away.

To me my duties at home were many. I had to milk, get the wood into the house, and sometimes clean the yard. I did not mind these duties very much though until some friend of mine came along and asked me to come play with him. Then there were many things that I could not do that when I wanted to I could do rather easily. When my mother asked me to wash dishes or sweep the floor, which was very seldom I suppose, (although it seemed to me very often then) I would usually refuse, but when I saw her go after the leather strap that she kept hanging in the dining room and used for purposes in which I was employed very frequently, I would usually be very busy washing dishes, sweeping the floor or whatever she told me to do, when she came back.

In the year of 1920, we moved to Uvalde in order to take advantage of the better school here and is the place we have lived ever since. My sister and I were to be in the seventh grade, but we were put back into the sixth because we had not as many studies as were required of a seventh grade student here. After a month in the sixth grade my sister made better grades than I did. The teacher let her go on into seventh grade or the freshman class as it was called here then. I did not like that very much, but as I did not have any say in what grade I was going to be I did not tell anyone of my sorrows. My only consolation was that my sister was one year and a half older than I and that I would be graduated when a little over sixteen years of age and she when a little over seventeen years of age.

When I was promoted to the freshman class and came up stairs I felt as though I had almost finished my high school education. I suppose all of us acted rather "green" because we were not accustomed to the study hall and having to go to different rooms for our classes. In spite of all our ignorance we did not like for anyone to tell us where to go or what to do next. Mr. Henderson was our general science teacher. On our first laboratory day we went to the chemistry room. We were going to make soap. Although very few of us succeeded in making soap, we had a delightful time. Our class made so much noise that Mr. Evans had to come in and "call the house to order." Our general science class went on several expeditions hunting insects, frogs and the like for our experiments. While I was in the sophomore class I made my first D on my report card. Father and Mother told me I had better get to studying because if I failed I would have to go to summer school and make up my grade. Since I did not like the idea of having to go to summer school, I got busy and made my low grades up to passing grade. The junior year was easy enough for me so I did not have any trouble in passing it. I am a senior now and if it was not for chemistry I believe I would pass through that class with a little effort.

An Interview of Blanche Brown Wright

by her daughter-in-law, Shirley Wright

You would have been nineteen when that house was built, right?

Yes, I was off at school. So when I got home–after I got–see they'd been living there a good—I guess when I came home after my junior year we were living there; because I stayed out a year. The year I taught in Cometa, which was, let's see what year 1927, I taught at Cometa School. And I was a junior–I mean I'd had two years, no I'd had three years 'cause I'd taken summers straight through.

Blanche

I'd started when I graduated from high school in '24, I went each summer and long terms—three summers and two long terms—so that made me ready for my senior year. And so, then I taught a year at Cometa–stayed out of school. And then, as soon as summer came, I went back to summer school and then I graduated long term. In '28, I graduated and by then we'd already moved back to the ranch.

But, when I taught in Cometa, we still lived in Uvalde then, 'cause Papa would come by once a month to pick me up at Cometa, which is on the west side of Crystal City, 14 miles, and then we'd drive to Uvalde for the weekend. So I got to go home once a month. And I made the stupendous amount of money of $85. And then that's when I boarded with the Harrises. Mr. Harris had been in the legislature so he felt that he was very knowledgeable–and he was a smart old man. And his wife–let's see how will I describe her—she was the—one of the trustees of the school where I taught. That's why I boarded with them. And the old man was a big tease. Where they lived they had a party line–fourteen people on the telephone. And the old man used to go ring the number and wait till he'd hear all the people take the phone off the hook to eavesdrop, and then he'd say, "Well, that'll be all, ladies," and hang up.

I'll always remember that about him. He was clever. And his old bachelor son that I've told you about, he was 45, was dating an English girl, who lived in that area, the Delamaine girl. And they really were English, so English that they wouldn't read the local paper. They sent to London for their papers. They were very British. But that year when they got married, I got to go to their wedding. We went to Eagle Pass for them to get married at the Episcopal Church.

No I said I met him and I believe he's teaching school—no I believe he was a bank director—I met him at Bernard's dance one Christmas. Maybe he was the son—I guess he was the son.

My home in the summer, but I never actually lived there because I'd already, was a working girl. I went off to teach in the long term. But, it was my home, see, to come to. My room was the boys' room. That was the fact. But to stay there a whole year, I never did you see, 'cause I'd already gone off to school.

Where was everyone else's room?

Jeanne's room was the middle room upstairs.

The green room?

Yes, the green room, where you all sleep. And downstairs—that was Hestel's room—the middle room.

The boys had the sleeping porch, the ones that didn't have a room—Paul and all outside guests. And the back—the horn room was Leslie's room. But, mostly the boys slept on the sleeping porch.

Bernard?

Bernard and Paul lived on the sleeping porch.

What about Aunt Norma?

Norma—let's see. Where was Aunt Norma? Gosh, she ought to be on that list.

She had the girls' room, maybe?

Wasn't any girls' room then. That was a big open room. Mama hadn't made that back room yet.

Well, unless she shared a room with Hestel, I don't remember. I guess she and Hestel had the middle room. But, see about that time, I taught one year in Rosenberg—that was '28–'29. Then, the next year, I went to Laredo. And I took Norma down there with me for her—to have a room, 'cause she was like me from there on—she went back home and stayed a year. I don't know if they ever used my room upstairs or not. I don't think anybody slept up in my room ever but me. So maybe Hestel went off to work. Maybe Norma stayed in Hestel's room, but that was always called Hestel's room. The reason that, for sure, that was Hestel's room, after we were married and gone, see, Hestel was still single, she was still home and that was always her room. So I'll have to ask Hestel where Norma headquartered, because Hestel lived at home longer than any of us did. She taught in the Batesville school.

Oh, did she? What age was she when she got married?

Well, I would guess she might have been 35. She wasn't very young. We thought she would never marry. We thought Leslie wouldn't marry either.

Now, how did she get to New Mexico, and how did she meet Uncle Doug?

She took a government test and let's see—was she up in San Antonio and when she took the test? I don't know, but she was teaching in that Mexican school even when I married. She was still teaching—after I was first married, she was still in the Mexican school. Then the next thing I know when the war came along, and they were offering government jobs, well she took a typing—a stenographer's job—bookkeeper or something and they shipped her out to Deming. You'll have to get the particulars on that from her.

What branch was she with?

You mean with Civil Service?

Was she with the military or was she on the base or something?

Yes, she was on the base in Deming. But I believe she worked in San Antonio a while before they sent her out there. I guess that was an air base, too. Now Doug's job at the air base—he was in transportation—shipping supplies back and forth, something like that. He was an expert at routing things??? Procuring, or something like that.

Now we haven't done anything really about your Uvalde school years—high school years.

Okay. When we got up to Uvalde, as I mentioned before—we entered the… they put us in the 7ᵗʰ grade. We hadn't had, nor did we expect a 7ᵗʰ grade. We thought we'd go into high school but they had eleven grades in Uvalde. So we entered the 7ᵗʰ grade together, but in one month's time they decided that I was—it was too easy for me, and they were going to put me in the freshman class. So I left my dear little brother—I left him very wistful as I walked out the door, and I felt very strange leaving him behind. But he got along very well without me. Pretty soon we'd see him carrying bouquets to his teachers. He got along all right. Up until then I used to point to him to raise his hand when I knew he'd know an answer. He would never recite because he was so timid. And then if I'd give him a nod he'd raise that little hand and answer the question. But I always heard his lessons at night. But, from there on I was big in Math and Spanish—that was my subject that I loved. I got along very well. I belonged to the Spanish Club. I did Interscholastic League Spelling in high school and grammar school in Batesville, and then when I got to Uvalde I spent all four years in spelling. They called it spelling and – used to be oral spelling when I first did it in grade school. By the time I got to Uvalde it became spelling and plain writing. They dictated the words. To determine whether a word was misspelled or not they isolated the letter and if it wasn't a true letter they called it a misspelled word. But anyway that was fun. As I've pointed out before, one of my spelling mates who was a year behind me in school was a minister's son. The Baptist Church was right across the street from the Catholic Church in Uvalde and the minister and his family—had ten— had a big, big family of boys, and Harlan was the one who spelled with me. And I liked him a lot—very good-looking boy. Later on he became a movie star known as Dana Andrews. He just died lately.

Oh, did he? I hadn't heard that.

But he was fun and we spelled together several years. We walked to high school from where we lived on High Street, we walked to school, which I thought was a pretty long walk. By today's standards it's wasn't too far, but it didn't hurt us a bit. We had two routes—we could either go down High Street and stay on the sidewalk, or we could cut through the back way and walk through an old cemetery, which was a more interesting route. And when we went that way and came out of the old cemetery, then we walked right down the street a few blocks by Garner's home. Vice-President Garner's home was on that street. We had a wonderful math teacher, and a wonderful Spanish teacher, both of them—very finest teachers. And I remember that Miss Bertha Dalton who inspired me as a Spanish teacher, and also English teacher—had a little car that had chains. I used to know the name of that funny little car but she drove everywhere in her funny little car that had chains over the tires. I can see those chains, but I can't think of the name of that car. But Miss Anthon later became County Superintendent, and when I finished college, she took me on a tour of the county trying to help me get a job when I was looking for work. She tried to place me up in Utopia, Garner Park—up in that area—all the county schools because she was in charge of them. But it ended up I took the school at Cometa. That was when I was a junior.

Now what sort of sports did you get involved in when you were in Uvalde?

Well, I had to play that softball, and Mama would not let—I loved basketball—but Mama would not allow me to go on out of town trips, so I never made any teams because I couldn't go out of town. See, in those days people were pretty strict, and Mama certainly wasn't going to let me go out of town 'cause she figured she couldn't go along to see what was going on because she had other children to take care of 'cause she's up there by herself. Papa's at the ranch. So I was never allowed to be on the first team on anything because I couldn't go out of town. But I was always allowed to play basketball and ???? We carried our lunch to school, too. And I took a year of Latin—I took Latin two years along with math and Spanish. I remember we had a teacher—let me see—I didn't know her in high school. She had taught there but when I got to the University I met this Spanish teacher who had taught in Uvalde, and because I had come from Uvalde High School, she sort of befriended me in college—took me out to lunch and things like that. As soon as I finished high school I begged

Mama to let me go on to school. Their heart was set on sending me to Our Lady of the Lake in San Antonio. But, I got their catalog, and I found out they didn't have summer school, and I persuaded Mama to let me go to the university because I found out I could stay with the Dominican Nuns. They had a convent called Newman Hall and I could be their boarder and go to school. So Mama said, "All right, just this summer."

So I went to Austin and started my work. Come September and I liked it so well, and there were so many nuns to take care of us and all, that I persuaded Mama 'why should I go to Our Lady of the Lake', I'm already up here?' But see I had a cousin named Nellie Mae—really Papa's cousin's daughter. Her name was Nellie Mae Kinnidge, but the daughter of Papa's first cousin. They'd always planned that we'd go to school together at our Lady of the Lake. Well, she went ahead and went to the Lady of the Lake, and I met her a few times, but we didn't ever become roommates at Our Lady of the Lake because I got my foot in the door at Austin, and I stayed there.

And what was your social life?

In the university?

No, in Uvalde.

In Uvalde? Well, I don't know that we had any social life in Uvalde. I guess you'd say our social life is: on the first Friday we'd carry our breakfast as well as our lunch, so we'd go by church and go to Mass on First Friday. And then, once a month, she gave us picture show money and we could go. If we'd go down to Benediction on Friday evenings we could go to the picture show afterwards. But, we took ourselves on our feet—we walked. And then, as we got a little older, we had some friends that had a car— boyfriends. I had two friends. They were cousins. They were rivals. They would offer me rides. But Mama had her mind on a certain boy that was in our church. She thought he'd be nice for me to go with, but I couldn't see it because he was a plumber's son. He was a plumber by trade. I didn't want to be caught dead with him—very stuck up—and anyway, one night Mama made me go to the show with him. You want this kind of trash?

Sure.

And I went to the show with him, but when we came out my boyfriend—
my two cousins had hot-wired his car. They put an electric button around
somewhere and had done something to his car. He never asked me for a
date again. 'Cause he knew who'd done it. And this woman was such a
nice—the mother of this boy—they went to our church and when we'd
go to benediction we'd be saying the rosary, she was very German and her
English wasn't so clear and she'd say, "bray for us, bray for us, bray for us."
And we'd sit back there and giggle, immediately behind her, you know, and
giggle. And we'd say "bray for us" too. Mama'd look at us and threaten
our lives, so forth, so on. We weren't exactly angels. Oh, yeah, and by then
love had hit me, and I'd get these notes. I'd get letters—not letters, notes.
And, oh, they were such nice notes. And I had to hide them because all my
devilish brothers and sisters would read them and quote them in front of
Papa and Mama at the supper table and that sort of thing. So I had pretty
good hideouts and I was—I wasn't allowed—I read so much that Mama
threatened my life. I couldn't bring anymore library books home. So it
forced me to get library books and put them in the barn. We had a hayloft
in that barn in Uvalde, too. So I'd keep my reading supply out there. But,
finally Mama got on it because my tattletale brother and sisters, like Paul
and Norma, told on me. And no matter where I'd hide my notes, they'd
find them and they'd quote them. Hestel was right in on it, too. She'd
help. They made my life miserable. First time anybody came to see me, I
was by then a senior in high school, why there was a friend from Utopia
who had this friend of her husband. She was going to bring him over and
introduce him because they thought he was such a nice man 'cause he was
their friend. And my brothers and sisters got on their hands and knees and
got under the curtain and shot peas at him as he sat on the sofa. But he
never came again--got rid of him.

It was very hard for me to have any friends like that socially. But, we did
play with the neighbors on the hill. We had moonlight—if it was a pretty
moonlight night, we'd go play on the hill. And the people that lived up
there were my two friends and their sisters.

What kind of games did you play?

What kind of games did we play? I guess kick the can. That's what we played. We could play in the moonlight. But it all passed very fast.

One of the things they did—sometimes they had a dance in Batesville at that old store which was then called 'The White Elephant'. And Mama was great on—and Papa—they thought we ought to go to the dance 'cause they wanted us to be interested in dancin', but neither one of us was very good. But Mama and Papa were so good, but I guess we were all thumbs—or all toes—I don't know which. Anyway, they let us go to Batesville to the dances. So sometimes Leslie and I would go to Batesville to the Friday night dance just a few times—I guess for social life.

And I remember after I graduated from college and came home and was 21 years old, and I was allowed to vote for the first time--Papa was holding the election and the question was should we move the courthouse to Crystal City or keep it in Batesville. And, of course, there were more Crystal Cityites than there were Batesvillians, so they won the election. But I got polled in that election—my first. It was the first year I voted.

Reminded me of how the family loved to come up to the ranch because it was so much fun. And see, even Norma, they'd all be my students and we'd play in the dining room. When I came home from school, I was going to teach them French. Annie Jay was laughing about that the other day. I was a big language hound. I was always going to teach something.

And let's say they wanted to go—Norma and Annie Jay wanted to go over to Crystal City to a stock show, I believe they were having. And Leslie and C. B. Ballard, who was a cousin of ours staying there, said they couldn't go. And we'd ask Leslie, "Where are you goin'?" He'd say, "Goin' to Chicago" or "I'm goin' to New York", but he never would say where he was goin'. Well, of course, we knew where he was goin'. So, Annie Jay reminded me of this not long ago. I do remember doing it. So we had a big tarp in the back of the truck, so when they were dressing and ready, I got my two little girls and put them in the back and put them under the tarp. They got over to Crystal City, and they raised up the tarp and surprise—they couldn't do a thing about it. They had 'em. And then one time, I did that. I wanted to go with them, and they said I couldn't go. This was before that even. And so I said, "Well, where you goin'?" I didn't want to go off 'cause I wanted to stay home and play dominoes or card games.

"Oh, they were goin' to New York."

So that was in our baby Opel. We had a baby Opel car. It didn't have a top on it. It had been taken off, and the car was right out the door.

And I thought, "You old fools. I'm goin' anyhow."

So I went down and squatted down between the seats. I wanted to see what they did. So they got over to Batesville and they drove around in the moonlight on the square. I didn't even have my shoes on. I let them know I'm there—they let me out in town, in the town square—me—a grown girl, you know—barefooted. And then finally, I didn't know what I was gonna do—I was stuck. Finally, they came back and picked me up and took me home. And I got out, and I didn't give them any more trouble.

Some thought young people shouldn't go to dances.

So, what kind of dances did they have?

Well, they had a fiddler and a violin and everybody far and near came. People from Dilley came out. All the young people came from surrounding counties and they had it in Batesville. Until Leslie told me I danced like a cow with a cob under my tail.

That didn't stop you did it?

Well, I believed him. I wasn't that hot a dancer. My mother was more interested in me dancing than I was, you know—in my dancing.

What else did we do? We played—on Friday nights sometimes-- we'd play up on the hill with the neighbors. We'd play kick the can. And, later when I graduated I immediately went off to the University of Texas to go to summer school. Then when the long term started, Mama let me stay there. They didn't send me to Our Lady of the Lake as they had originally planned because they found out that the Dominican nuns would take good care of us where we were, so I stayed at Newman Hall, while in my college career. And I went to the University summer and winter and stayed out my junior year to teach school, and I taught in Cometa one year and then went on back to school and graduated in 1928.

And what kind of degree?

Well, a BA in—major in Spanish and minor in French and Italian.

And where did you get your math?

Well, I had to have two years—I had two years of math because I had advanced standing from high school in solid geometry. And then I had a year of math—I had trig and analyt and college algebra.

Did you have kind of a degree in math, though?

No. But also I had five years of education. I was well prepared to teach. And I had a high school diploma as well as grammar school—the right to teach anywhere. And I had a lifetime teaching certificate when I graduated.

But you did finally get a degree in math, right?

Yeah. Well, when I went back to get my masters many years later—well, before that I went to—I took a correspondence course when it was obvious that I was living in Laredo where they didn't need me to teach Spanish— well, then, they put me to teaching math from the beginning. So I just took a correspondence course. I took "Pure Mathematics of Finance". That's six hours by correspondence. Then I went to junior college and took calculus, and then I took—half of my calculus by correspondence, and half of it in junior college. And then I went off to Hays, Kansas one summer with a government grant. They wanted us to prepare to teach modern math. So I took advantage of that and I got—I went two summers under that, so that's when I was well taught by—I didn't ever get a degree as such in math, but I had more than enough credits. I had many hours of math. I don't remember now how many, but nobody questioned my ability—my right to teach math—because of the many credits I had.

And, when I went—all those years, I was taking courses that were offered in Laredo by the University of Texas. They'd come down there and offer a course. I'd take it. So I had six hours of Spanish History, because I took Latin American History. It was tied in with both majors, you see. And then I took—I'm talking about some of the correspondence courses—I took an education course that had to do with teaching of Spanish, and I took—some of it counted as residents credit although it really wasn't—it was offered there—but they gave me six hours residents' credit. So in 1949, I'd been married a good while. So when Mary Paul was about three I went back to the University, and I wrote my thesis—I already had all the credits I needed—I wrote my thesis and took a year of—let's see what did I have to do—I think I had to take six more hours of math. I took statistics. They counted that as math. Anyway I got my BA degree again. I had a major in Spanish and English and a minor—well, I don't know if they gave me—I don't know if it mentioned math. I've forgotten if it did or not, but I was well qualified in math. I think as I recall it was a Master of Education degree is what they called it—Master of Education. But it was in English—see I had taken Shakespeare and a lot of other courses in between. I don't know how many college credits I had. I had more than enough for a Masters when I got my mine. But I believe it was called a Master of Education degree.

Do you want to tell us about any of your antics when you were in college?

Well, of course, we loved to swim, and sometimes we were so broke—we'd want to go to the show—my dear friend, Erin and I. There was a girl in university I didn't particularly like. She had her own car as a freshman; I thought she was kind of coarse, and I didn't particularly like her. But, I'd go down the hall and somebody would say, "You got a letter", and I'd go down and I wouldn't have a letter. She'd have a letter. And people would— teacher would—saw her on the campus—saw me on the campus—and told me that I passed my German—well, I wasn't taking German. And people were mistaking us, and it was decided that we looked so much alike they didn't know us, so became—to like each other—and became twins—bosom friends and twins. We weighed the same, were the same height—only thing, while I'm taking Spanish, she's taking German. And, we were mistaken for each other so many times that we really became very close friends. From there on we were inseparable. We had many pictures showing our similarity. And that was Erin from Galveston. And one year, in summer school, we went down to Galveston and spent the 4th of July with her folks. After I'd been married ten years, she brought her children and came to Laredo and visited us. We went to Monterey and to Saltillo and Horsetail Falls. Edward took us. And then, I took my twins and Mary Paul one summer and went to Galveston and visited her. I thought that interesting. And the year that we went from the university down there, we took several friends, and one of them was the sister to Mrs. Billy Holsworth, who is the sister to Mrs. HEB (H.E.Butt, who was a friend of our family's.) And I had run into her at the university, and she'd become a very close friend because of her connection with the Batesville Holsworths. Paul and Hestel had been big friends with their Aunt Kate. So we took Billy Holsworth who was a grown girl, much older than we were, but she went down there with us and she had the best time she ever had in her life. She was—I guess a college teacher herself there in the University. I recall that I joined a Spanish sorority. It was for scholastic standing. I think it was called Sigma Delta Pi. It was honorary Spanish; and then I belonged to a Spanish club when I was in the University. And I didn't like it.

I had a boyfriend when I was a freshman. He was kind of fat, but he had a fine car. He had a—I don't remember now—Chrysler I guess—some kind of a big car. I've forgotten what the name of it was. I was the envy of the dorm because my fat friend lived there, and I had transportation when I wanted to go places, and my friends could go along. And, let's see, what else.

We sometimes took train excursions over to San Antonio on a Sunday just to eat Mexican food at the Mexican restaurant—the Original Mexican Restaurant there on Navarro Street. And let's see if I remember any other exciting things. No, I think all the excitement was that I stayed out my junior year and taught at Cometa and you have an article on that in the file somewhere. And that helped me.

After I graduated, a cattle buyer came out to the ranch and offered me a job down at Rosenberg, Texas. He was one of the trustees of the school. He offered me this job and I took it, and the only reason I got to be the principal and the high school teacher was because I had a degree and the other teachers who had been working there for a good many years were under me. Can you imagine? I didn't even know how to start a coal fire. They burned coal in their fire. And I taught all the high school subjects—grouped them together.

It didn't last but eight months, it wasn't a nine-month school. But I was glad to take the train and go home. I spent most of my weekends going back. I'd ride into town with Miss Gephardt who lived in the town of Rosenberg—see this was a consolidated rural school, and they had many narrow lanes and cotton trucks would turn – the angles were so sharp—sometimes they'd turn over at the corner there by the schoolhouse, and the bales of cotton would be on the ground. Everything was King Cotton out there in those days.

The understanding was that the people I boarded with would take me to school when it rained. It rained all the time and they'd look out, and they'd say, "It's not very muddy. It's not raining." So I had to walk. You'd take one step forward and slip back two. It was terrible, and I had rubbers, but they'd come off and my shoes would come off in that old black mud. It was horrible. I wouldn't have gone back down there for anything in the world.

When that year was out I went back up to Draughon's Business College and took business college courses. And they gave me a lifetime scholarship to Draughon's Business College because I could help them with the teaching. So I taught Business English and Business Spelling in return for my lifetime scholarship. And so, two different summers I went to Draughon's Business College. I took shorthand, business math—rapid calculation they called it, bookkeeping—combined course it was called.

What was your next teaching job?

Well, then at the end of summer I was not going back down to Rosenberg. I thought I'd just stay and work and go to Business College. They got me a job in a drug store which was part of the college. See there the deal was that you had to work. All the students worked to get on-the-job training, and they got you a job, and then you went to school. My job was two hours at night in a drug store there in San Antonio. The drug store was on Pecan Street I remember. And right next door to that was a great big garage, and the owner came over to buy his cigars every evening about 8:00and he was a nice man—a big tall fellow, I remember—a German guy. He always liked to show off a little because he spoke Spanish. When I sassed him—gave him a little answer a time or two—then he got to teasing me, and one day he came over at the end of the summer, and he wanted to know if I would consider going to Laredo because he had a garage—a branch garage there. The manager didn't speak a word of Spanish, he wasn't collecting the bills, and would I go down there and be the assistant to the manager and collect the bills. He'd furnish the car and all if I'd collect the bills and write up a report.

But, anyway, I went down there and by the time school started obviously the report that I had to make, and I did my collecting, it didn't take very long to collect the bills that were collectible.

You actually went around and collected the bills?

Yes, I actually went around. He loaned me a car, and I went around. Well, anyhow, I did that and, because I could speak Spanish, I guess I was a help to the manager. And, then when school started, I decided that I wasn't going to—I could do that after school—that report I had to make. Every day I had to make this report—a form to fill out. So I had to make the report in two hours, and I said I can do that after school. So they let me go back to teaching.

I went to the Superintendent, Mr. Everhart, and got a job teaching, and I've been teaching ever since. I kept that job as part time working Saturdays and after school for three or four years.

Now where was the job where you used to have to cross the pasture? Where was that?

Oh, that—when I was teaching at Cometa. Oh, yes. I had to walk quite a distance—it seemed to me like three miles, but I guess it wasn't over two. I boarded with the Harris family, and I had to cross a creek. First though I had to cross a pasture. It was fenced in barbed wire. I had to cross two fences to get to the road. The boogarboo was the Brahma bull—big old, purple, huge thing that no fence could stop it. So my idea was to sneak through without being seen, and of course that probably gave me a nervous indigestion nearly—that, plus the fact that we had a jigger of Crowder peas every day of the year. That whole year—when that year of teaching at Cometa was over, I had to go to San Antonio to be treated for nervous indigestion. Mama sent me up there every Saturday on the bus for treatment because either it was the food or the tension of crossing—I don't know which.

What I started to say about crossing, after I went under the path I'd escaped the Brahma bull, then I crossed the road under a bridge, and as I'd go under the bridge I'd hear "shissss". I'd die nine deaths, and it happened two or three times. I just got to where I expected it. But I didn't know what in the world was going on. Finally I discovered a big old bird, old owl, I guess, a hawk or something—sittin' up on the banisters of the bridge, overhead, and that was what was hissing at me as I'd go under the bridge.

Then I had to walk through the pasture to one of the trustee's house to get her little girl who had started to school that year, and I'd take her little hand and went on up the hill to the schoolhouse. And some days, I'd have four students. Some days, I wouldn't have anyone but little Mary Jane, who was my beginning student. And I taught her so much because she was the only pupil there—nobody was going to catch me leaving the grounds during the school hours. I stayed up there so I'd be sure they paid me my money. I wasn't going to give it to them.

And, one of the things if nobody came—if Mary Jane had a toothache and the other students didn't show, I found out that they had old window panes under the floor of the schoolhouse and they had red dirt up there, red sand and ochre, you could find yellow color, you could find a lot of pigments in the sand. And, I'd get mesquite glue and melt it on the stove and paint on this glass. I thought I was doing oil painting. And I'd paint. I'd put glue on first and then I'd press all these designs. I made some real pretty designs, and I even imprinted the leaves on that – stuck it to the glass. And it was something to do—to spend the day. I didn't have anything to read. I'd just stay up there, so I did.

And it was customary to have any social function that was held, at the schoolhouse. So sometimes on Friday nights, they'd have a dance there. The whole—all the families would go: father, mother, brother, sister—everybody.

But, at the most, I guess there must not have been over – maybe not even thirteen students. I don't know how many pupils there were, but mostly maybe four would come, maybe one or two, and maybe none. But there was a family named English supposed to be there all the time, but they didn't always come because they had to come quite a distance. I think I've told all of that in my episode of teaching at Cometa.

Once a month I got to go home, I think I told that too. Papa would come by and pick me up. The reason I got to go home once a month was to deposit my check.

So did you ever narrowly escape the bull?

No, no. I never narrowly escaped the bull. I finally saw him and I knew his—what they said was not to let him see me.

But it seems to me like when we did your file there were lots of little places – towns – that you taught. Is that not true or did I just imagine it?

No—I taught—see, I taught in Rosenberg. First, I taught that—when I was a junior—I taught at Cometa. And then, I taught—after I got my degree—I taught down here at Rosenberg in Cottonwood Consolidated School, it was called. It was about six miles out of Rosenberg to the south somewhere. Then I taught at Laredo. But, I taught in the Heights School in Laredo. I taught the second grade the first year that I got the job. And then the next year at Christen School which is a junior high, and they moved me there. I taught there several years until—see I was married—the year Tony was born, I stayed home until—let's see, he was born in February and then I—after a few months I went back to work. I got this job at Montgomery Ward as a bookkeeper, and I was teaching after school and on Saturdays. And I did that for several years, until after Mary Paul was born, I worked for them.

Now, why don't we talk about your life in Laredo and how you met Daddy?

The day that Mr. Kalise took me down to Laredo—Mr. Ula it was. It was Ula and Kalise was the name of the garage, and it was called UK Garage. But the night that Mr. Ula took me down there he got me a room in the Plaza Hotel.

The next morning, the next day, I called my cousin, Nora, who lived down there. I had two cousins living there—Vivian Carroll, and Nora Dunn. Nora was married already and so they came and got me as soon as work was over and took me driving to see the family. And they slammed on the brake right down at the corner of Convent and Matamoros. There stood Edward. First time I ever saw him. And they called him, "Huesos, come here." That was Edward's nickname. It means bones. So Huesos came over and they introduced us, and it turned out Huesos was their good friend— Nora and Harold's good friend. And, the next morning when I got up to go to work I saw Leo, and I spoke to him. I thought it was Edward. And he ignored me. He didn't speak to me. He worked for the gas company, which was right there in the part of the same building where I was. But he didn't speak, and I thought—so that evening when Edward called me for a date, I said, "Indeed not. You couldn't even speak to me after I spoke to you."

Blanche's Eightieth Birthday Party Roast

We are honored that Mom came—she gave up a Delta Kappa Gamma party to be with us.

Mom protested when we started planning this party. She said she'd been beatified twice—once when she retired and once when they had the 50th anniversary of Martin High—and she didn't want any more such ceremonies.

Well we wanted to have a party for her, and we said, "If she doesn't want to be beatified, fine."

So, Mom, we talked to your brothers and sisters—nieces and nephews—sons and daughter—and your grandchildren. And, we dug some dirt—stirred up a few ashes—and I just believe we can roast you instead.

Let's go back to your early years.

Just like Abraham Lincoln, Mom has always been an avid reader. Sometimes, however, a little reading was a dangerous thing.

HESTEL (Sister)

When she was a young girl, one of her early chores was ironing everything—including the BVDs. She sat on a stool and read a book while she ironed. She would get to going back and forth as she read so that she traditionally scorched the shirts. More than once her sisters had to back into a classroom in school so their friends wouldn't see the scorch mark on the front of their dresses.

Here's a memento of one of those days. BOX NO. 1

Now let's talk about our childhood in Laredo. Growing up in Laredo was a very special thing—you had to be special to survive. One of the things we all survived—and are no doubt better for—was Mom's system of discipline.

Normally, Dad meted out the punishments. Mom would usually wait till he got home before we had to go out to the athol tree, select a suitable switch, and present it. And, Lord help you if you didn't select a proper switch (include what happened if you didn't). Then it was off to the washroom for a dance around the washing machine. Most people learn to dance at dancing school—I learned in the washroom. Did you ever wonder where the Schottische originated?

I never realized until I was a grown man having a suit fitted, and the tailor pointed it out to me. One shoulder was higher than the other—no doubt from being held up by my arm while I danced around the washing machine. (Demonstrate)

A few years later the system of punishment was revised when Uncle Floyd gave us a pony and we got a quirt to go along with it. With this new weapon in hand, Mom came into her own. I was the only one in the family to be punished in that manner. Mary Paul says she got it with a ruler, but if she ever got spanked, I never saw it.

It wasn't that we didn't have our protectors. Granny would always call from across the street to see what was wrong if I yelled loud enough. Mike, too, can offer a testimonial to the days of Athol switches and red legs.

MIKE

(The twins had Santos on site to protect them. They were smarter than me, too. They would go climb up the slim branches of the Athol tree whenever they were sent to select a switch. They couldn't be reached by Mom, and they would stay up till she agreed not to switch them or Santos came to rescue them

"Pobrecitos," she would say (poor little kids).

PAT

Of course, Mom would wait till Dad got home. He could get them out of the tree. Mary Paul never got spanked, so she had no need of protection!

And, Mom and Santos always had a thing going to determine who really ran the household and the twins. I frequently voted for Santos when she made beans, rice and enchiladas.

Side note: You need to understand that, in this world, beans rice and enchiladas is really three dishes, but all one word.

Tony:

When I was a teenager, I suspected for a while that Mom came from the planet Krypton because she had Superman-like senses—at least in her hearing and smell—and she was the only person I ever knew who sleeps with one eye open. She always knew when I came in the back door at night, and—from her bed—she was able to tell what I had had to drink and what I had smoked. I can hear her saying, "Have you been smoking again," or "Is that beer I smell on your breath?" Unfortunately, I married a person with the same senses.

The twins were always suspect of wetting the bed, even as they got a little older. So, whenever Mom woke up she took them to the bathroom. When I came in at night, she would automatically wake up and tell me to take them to the bathroom. I was sure that if ever a burglar came in, she would insist he take the twins to the bathroom before he robbed the house.

The cure for all illness was castor oil. We knew that if we stayed home from school it would mean we got a dose of castor oil. We never faked—you really were sick when you would put up with that.

It's a wonder Mary Paul ever got married because Mom had a very low tolerance for her dates. The twins would squirt water guns at them when they came to call. The twins say Mom set it up.

In fact, her penchant for running off unwanted suitors goes back many years. I understand one of Aunt Norma's serious beaus donated an engagement ring to Mom after she managed to engineer the demise of their romance.

Well, Mom, you are such a many-faceted person, we have barely scratched the surface. But there's one quality we can't overlook as it is exhibited simultaneously with so many of your other talents. Your frugality is legend. Right, Mary Paul?

MARY PAUL – In my early memories, I can still see a pile of old newspapers in our home in Laredo. They were always there. I have no idea why they were there or what we did with them, but I'm sure you kept them for some good reason.

She is the only person I know who actually goes to the bank to be sure they pay the interest on her CD's when they come due. She also has to be in town to pay her bills each month. The post office must refuse to accept them if they are mailed anywhere but Laredo.

However, there are many other areas where she exhibited a thrifty nature. When we were growing up, she cooked original meals on Sunday only. She added different vegetables or combined the week's dishes in different culinary delights the rest of the week.

Mary Paul remembers her steaks most fondly.

MARY PAUL – She was especially adept at cooking steak well done. About the third time she served the steaks that week, they were so well cooked we all learned to eat vegetables and enjoy them.

Some cousins, who lived with Mom and Dad for a while, tell the tale about her Saturday night specials.

Each Saturday they were sent to the tortilla factory to get tortillas. She would put out a layer of tortillas - Monday's meal - another layer of tortillas - Tuesday's meal, and so on until they had a review of the entire week. Pat and Mike didn't like it but Tissie and Doonie called it Aunt Blanche's Saturday Surprise.

We have obtained a copy of the original recipe which reads as follows:

AUNT BLANCHE'S SATURDAY SURPRISE

(This version has been adapted for use at any time.)

First, grease large Dutch oven

Layer 1 – Fresh tortillas

Layer 2 – Leftover from meals six days past

Layer 3 – Fresh tortillas

Layer 4 – Leftovers from meal five days past

Continue in this manner until you have added yesterday's meal and a final layer of tortillas.

(If necessary, you may add another layer consisting of any stray leftovers from this week's breakfast or snacks.)

OR

If necessary, to conclude a meal hastily, you may insert a layer of chocolate cake or peach cobbler ingredients.

Disguise all with 1 gallon mixture of tomato puree and water – highly seasoned with cumin and cilantro.

Bake until hot.

Serve with a great show of confidence in order to discourage dissenters.

(Copies of this recipe are available on request.)

Mary Paul's kids remember her thrift in other ways.

ERIN   Tells of Mom saving the leftover milk from their cereal bowls to bake cookies with.

Mom, we are aware that cleaning your refrigerator always endangers many valuable leftovers. So the next time you decide to clean it, here's a gift to help you get going again.

REFRIGERATOR STARTER GIFT KIT

Contents

2 – DAB JARS PRETREATED WITH BEARDS
(1 Clean, 1 with beans)
2 – SEASONED ORANGES
1 - PACKET AGED CHEESE (WITH MOLD STARTER)

BOX NO. 6

From the earliest days, Mom stretched the dollar with her sewing. She made suits and tuxedos, shirts from flour sacks by cutting a hole for the head and arms, and there was always an unlimited supply of handkerchiefs, which she made by cutting up old sheets. She was a world-class seamstress.

PAT   Right. She actually taught Maria Von Trapp some of her thrifty sewing tricks. Remember the scene in "The Sound of Music" where Julie Andrews takes down the drapes in her room to make play clothes for the children? Mom actually originated that idea when she made playsuits for the twins from curtain material—bright green and white. She made school knapsacks for the twins, and when the twins wouldn't use the knapsacks she made clothespin carriers out of them. She also turned the material into Mary Paul's senior prom dress. (Ballerina costumes for party.)

SHIRLEY And when we say "Where is that darned dishcloth? We really mean it." (A mended dishcloth.)

Mary Paul was probably the beneficiary of most of her sewing. She took Dad's old worn out pants and made skirts for Mary Paul. The worn spots were still apparent.

Now that we've maligned your virtues, let's attack your vices.

As far back as I can remember Mom had a passion for gambling, especially poker. When I called Roddy Notzon to ask if he had any early day memories of Mom, he said it was the poker games she played in. It was before my time, and she had the passion then. I remember Dad would never play with her. I couldn't understand why till I started playing with her a few years later.

Her rules are slightly different from most anyone else's. In canvassing the family for information about her card background, I found that she learned canasta (the conventional type), then changed to California rules when she went out there and found rules which suited her style of play better. We had to set up rules for when she came to visit in order to have half a chance to compete. So, we wound up playing with "East of the Brazos" rules when we went camping at Sam Rayburn, and "West of the Brazos" rules when we were in her territory.

Mary Paul shared a few memories with me.

MARY PAUL – *"Mom always had a penchant for peeking at the card in the stack accidentally, but always practices stewardship of her opponent's honesty. Her peek is your cheat. She is a virtuoso at demonstrating righteous indignation when you mention that she may not be playing in accordance with the rules."*

The penchant for gambling was very evident a few years back when Mary Paul was expecting them to come see her after a two-week to Disneyland and California. They dropped out of sight for three weeks. It seems they only got as far as Las Vegas.

I understand the casinos doubled the table watchers while she was there.

Another favorite ploy at the card table is to feign sleepiness whenever her hands don't measure up to her standards. Suddenly, she just can't keep her eyes open!

Perhaps someone could explain to us why she gambles under the stage name of Herman. I understand that is has something to do with a technique she learned after WW2. (The remark implies she concealed cards as did Herman Goering conceal poison prior to his suicide).

Perhaps her tricks at the card table were the beginnings of her world travels. When you play cards like she does, you'd better be ready to move on fast.

I remember when Tim was born. Mom came to Wisconsin to help out. That was a big milestone in her life. She rode up with Aunt Dorothy, but in order to get home she had to fly for the first time. Only her first grandchild could have caused her to take that first step. Since then she has become a world traveler. And her traveling companions also attest to the fact that she is a world-class worrier.

AUNT DOROTHY is an eyewitness.

She reported that Mom never sees half the things she is supposed to on the tours because she is so worried she will not be the first one back to the tour bus. She has a phobia about losing her luggage. She did actually lose her suitcase and umbrella in Okinawa once, which probably justified all her anxiety over the years.

MARY PAUL

Once when Mary Paul and Don met them at Heathrow airport a porter tried to pick up her luggage and take it to their car. As she greeted them, she shouted, "Don, grab that man. He's stealing my luggage." The poor porter was terrified.

Incidentally, I don't know whether it's a result of traveling or just her nature, but she is the only person in St. Peter's parish—where there hasn't been a new person in the church in the last 5 years—who takes her purse when she goes to communion.

To go on a camping or touring trip with her and Aunt Hestel is always entertaining. If you haven't had the experience of watching her direct the parking and leveling of the camper you haven't seen animation in its highest form. You always had to check out every spot on the campground. Mom used to deposit a different grandchild at every likely campsite till she found one that suited. Then, unless you wanted to take your life in your hands, it was best to sit under a tree and stay out of the way while she directed the parking.

We all know that this is Mom's 80th birthday. Now, they say you're only as old as you feel, but Mom is trying to change that to 'you're only as old as your parts'. Here lately she's been undergoing a complete rebuilding of a lot of her parts. Her new neck arteries, eyes and ears are just a few parts, which make her as good as or better than her teen years.

Her bossiness, however, is still original. Aunt Hestel tells me that Mom was so authoritarian when they were children that she was a grown woman before she knew that everything Mom said wasn't gospel.

It would be unthinkable for her to be second in command in any situation. I always felt it was her willpower, which allowed her to float like a cork on any body of water. She amazed many a youngster with her levitation act. We've watched little kids edge up to her and bump her just to see if they can make her fall off her "invisible" float.

Some questions

Have you always read murder mysteries?

What did you do with the papers on the back porch of our house?

Why do you have to be in town to pay bills?

Actually, we wouldn't kid you if we didn't know your real nature—that of a generous, loving mother, sister, aunt and grandmother who has given us all an example of how to be a real human being, while still having a good time.

Thanks, Mom.

Park Family

An article handwritten by Blanche Brown Wright

(This article was the basis for the novel "Todos Santos." It was Mary Cecil Park Brown's belief throughout her life. In recent years the story of the parent's death and subsequent children's separation was proven to be incorrect.

A Mr. & Mrs. Park, (1st names not available) with their 4 small children, sailed from Scotland in early 1852. During the voyage Mr. and Mrs. Park became deathly ill and some say that they were buried at sea, while others contend that they died and were buried after they landed in Texas (Indianola). Whatever the case, the 4 young children were left orphans. David Park, born April 6, 1845 and William Park, born in 1850 (I'd heard Grandpa was 8 mos. old), were taken by the Ridgeway family to Leon County. In 1856, the Ridgeway family moved to Frio County where the Park boys were to grow up and spend the rest of their days. What became of the older two Park children, Archibald and Lillian, is not known. It was thought they were taken back to Scotland by a family that knew them and were with them on the boat coming over.

The following was discovered after Mary Cecil's death.

Park Family Story...what really happened.

This interpretation is made from Mrs. Wood's letter, which was emailed from Scotland to a DAR website in US. It is not known who sent it from Scotland.

William and Frances (Smith) Park who were born in Lanarkshire, Scotland came to the United States with four children in 1851 arriving 4/28/1851 on either the vessel John Gannon or Olympus. (Both vessels are shown on the port of New Orleans arrival list.) It is known the Olympus suffered severe damage in a storm and passengers could have been transferred to the John Gannon, thus two boats shown.

Interestingly, the departure location is Liverpool, not Greenock, Scotland, the usual Scottish departure sight. My assumption is they were both sailing vessels. A subsequent paddlewheel boat was taken to Galveston. From Galveston, a party of 31 led by a Mr. Ballantyne and Capt. Mc Kenzie rode up the Trinity River on a paddleboat to More's Bluff, Navarro County. They camped beside Mr. More's farm for two weeks while waiting for horses and wagons bought in Houston. Presumably they then moved on toward land they had purchased. Will Park died in route on June 12th at a Mr. Lamb's farm in Leon County. I have not located that farm on the old maps. He was apparently healthy and worked a few days between June 1st and June 12th. Frances Park cut her finger on a fishbone but was otherwise healthy at that time.

Frances apparently fell and died shortly thereafter. Her death may have been from the fall. The letter is unclear but David and Billy were taken to raise by Mr. and Mrs. Ridgeway. I have assumed this is James and Corilla Ridgeway. Emma Ridgeway was an adoptive sister of my great grandfather Billy Park (William's son) who visited him on his deathbed. Archibald Park grew up with the Wood Family in Hill County, in 1861 enlisted in Parsons Texas Cavalry, served until August 1864 in Louisiana when he was captured. He was sent to a Union prison in Elmira New York, the worst prison on either side. 2400 of 12000 prisoners died there. Archie was paroled at James River Virginia, and ended a few days later in Richmond where he died of chronic dysentery April 1865.

Lillias also lived with the Wood family. Mrs. Wood's maiden name was Ferguson. Her nephew John M Ferguson came to visit and ended up marrying Lillias. They had one son, William Park Ferguson, and a daughter, Emily. Emily and Lillias died within a month of each other in 1872 and are buried together in Wilford, Texas cemetery. John Fitzgerald took his son Will to Pike County, Arkansas where he remarried and had several more children.

William Park Fitzgerald lived his life in Pike County. He married, but no contact has been made with his children.

(Resuming Blanche's story)

The Ridgeways eventually settled at the old Martin Settlement, about 15 miles NW of Dilley near the Leona River. David and Billy (my grandpa) were in the area during the fateful Indian raid on July 4, 1865. Some of the settlers of the vicinity were the Martins, Odens, Franks, Bennetts, Levi English, Ed Burleson, Park and Hays families. The rancher plans for a big July 4 celebration were abrogated when Ed Burleson was attacked by Indians while out looking for horses. Warning the others brought a deadly hot pursuit by eleven of the ranchers. The Indians, numbering 32, were able to kill three of the settlers, and put the rest in fast retreat, some looking like the backside of a porcupine with arrows sticking out of them. The ranchers on the Leona had been about as reckless as Custer some years later on the Little Big Horn.

One of the men killed in the short-lived battle was Dean Oden. Dean, a young rancher, left his wife, Caroline Hay Oden (b.10/29/1841) with 2 small sons, Lewis and Sam. The young widow and David Park were married April 11, 1869, nearly 4 years after the battle. Their children are: Royal Silas (Sie) born 3/2/1870; Wm. Archie, Nov. 27, 1872; Frank L., October 11, 1874; John B., Jan. 12, 1877; and Ora L., Nov. 23, 1882. (These were Mama's first cousins and close neighbors.)

In the summer of 1876 David Park bought several hundred acres on Todos Santos Creek, near what became later Divot. This became the "home place" from which he, with his boys, ran the cattle operations. This was prior to the fences and, like most other ranchers, his cattle ran over most of the area that is now Frio and LaSalle Counties.

Mrs. David Park died at the Park ranch home 1/28/1898. Since David and the four Park boys were busy with ranch work, they thought it best to send 15 year old Ora off to Mary Hardin Baylor, rather than have her be at the ranch by herself.

In 1898, Wm. Archie married Fannie Rumfield. They had Walter Archie, Oliver, Virgil and Harold. Wm. Archie died from the flu 1917. His oldest son, Walter Archie, married Hattie Halsell, a Frio County girl. They had 2 children: Billie Ruth Solansky, who lives on the Nueces River between Crystal City and Carrizo Springs, and William Archie Park, who is a Baptist missionary to the Spanish in Roma, Texas.

"Sie" Park married Miss Bettie Ward in 1902 and ranched until retirement in 1942. Sie and Bettie were teachers. Sie taught Mary Cecil Park (his cousin). Sie died 1958. John died 1947. Frank lived in Frio County all his 94 years—died 1968 in Dilley. David, the Scotsman, the orphan, the rancher, continued to live on his Frio County ranch until his death August 10, 1911.

After a couple of years at Mary Hardin Baylor Miss Ora returned to Frio County where she lived to be 100.

Mary Cecil Park Brown

Mary Cecil Park Brown

Handwritten by Blanche Brown Wright, Transcribed by Shirley Wright

Mary Cecil Park was born October 1, 1885, in Frio County, Texas, near the Todos Santos Creek. She was the sixth of eight children of Mr. and Mrs. William Park. Her mother was born Mary Elizabeth Mudd in Louisville, Kentucky, April 6, 1851, (one of 12 children). Her father, William Park, was born January 12, 1850, in Glasgow, Scotland. Her parents probably met in San Antonio or Somerset, Texas and were married in the early 1870's.

She grew up in a family of five children; two girls had died at birth and a little brother, Lister, died at age two from diphtheria. (His was the second burial in the Pearsall Cemetery, where Mom's parents are buried.

Mom relates the following in speaking of her school days:

"In my school days we attended a one-room, one-teacher school. The school term generally lasted three or four months—depending on the amount of money the community could get together. (This was before the time of state-supported schools). We were about 20 or fewer students. My first teacher was my cousin, Si Park, who had been educated at Sam Houston Normal, Huntsville, Texas. The desk was one long table with benches on each side—the students faced each other. Several years later we got real desks. Water was from a hand-dug well on the school ground. We all drank from a common dipper. The ringing of the school bell brought a rush to the well for a last quick drink—and possibly for a quick dunk to cool off. In winter we kept warm by burning mesquite wood in an iron heater. Our transportation was by horseback or by wagon; the distance traveled to school was about three miles. We had to get up at four a.m. in order to get the horses and feed them before time to leave for school. My brother, Willie's job was to feed to horses.

The students were graded by the number of readers they read. The readers were numbered from 1 to 5, but were re-read time and time again in one school term. After we finished the readers, we studied geography, spelling, physiology and grammar. We had copybooks for writing. We studied both Texas history and then U.S. history. We had arithmetic all along, from the second grade. Later on, we had geometry which, for me, a nice pastime, but of little use. In grammar we had diagramming.

Among later teachers I recall were Miss Anece Burden (later Mrs. Harry Hornsby), a Mr. Beasley, a Miss Irene Rogers and a Mr. Hatsfield. Later on, I was sent to San Antonio where I attended Marshall Street School and lived with my mother's sister, Mrs. Lee Porter, on Cadwallader Street across the San Pedro (ditch). We crossed N. Flores Street to get to school.

I had two older brothers, George, born Mayo 16, 1875, and Jay, born August 15, 1882. Willie, my baby brother was born March 25, 1888. Later, he married Miss Eunice Williams and ranched on the Williams ranch between La Pryor and Eagle Pass. Jay probably attended school in Pearsall. As a young man, he went to work for the Southern Pacific Railroad as a water inspector. His wife was Eva Parten of San Antonio (Charlie's cousin). They had one son, Edwin, now living in Sacramento, California. Willie attended the Leona School with us. He later went to work in the copper mines in Arizona and finally became a surveyor. He came of retirement age and retired as a civil engineer from the Gas Co. of California. Willie's widow, Roberta, still lives near Osborne, California. Willie had two children, a daughter, Joyce Cecil (deceased), and Jay Jr, now living near his mother in California. My sister Norma attended the Leona school and later the Ursuline Convent in San Antonio. She married Charley's brother Milton. Charley and Milton attended schools in Halletsville and later were sent to the St. Louis College (now St. Mary's in San Antonio. Milton and Norma had three children, Vincent, San Antonio, and Annie Jay, (Mrs. Benton Roberts) of Pearsall, Cecil Muriel (Fritz), Mrs. Billie Staudt of San Antonio, Texas.

Charles Andrew Brown and Mary Cecil Park were married May 30, 1905, Tuesday, at three p.m. at her home by Reverend Father Leon Monastaire of San Antonio, Texas. Father came by train to Dilley and was met by Harmon Rummel and brought to my home. As soon as the ceremony was over, Harmon took the priest back to Dilley.

Present at the wedding were family, Norma, Willie, my parents; the Si Park family and the grooms parents, Mr. and Mrs. Bernard Brown and sister Viola and Mr. and Mrs. Jim Carroll (Aunt Ada). Immediately after the ceremony the bride and groom left in a borrowed buggy (Mr. Carpenters), but with Charley's own horses. We arrived at the ranch east of Batesville at midnight.

Our house consisted of one long room with one end petitioned off to be our kitchen and dining room. The furniture was a dresser, two chairs, a rocker and a washstand, the one now in the upstairs east bedroom The bed was the one now called the "rock of Gibraltar" at the west end of the sleeping porch.

It had a feather bed mattress and two pillows. The mattress and two pillows had been made from feathers from the Brown family's Halletsville geese. Feathers from that mattress were later used in making pillows for my children as they married.

The rocker broke down in later years when John Maddox sat in it. There was a wood stove, no electricity and no running water. There was a dug well near our house. Water was hand drawn and carried into the kitchen. Charley had a hired hand that helped him on the ranch. When Charley went off to get married and the hired hand was left in charge, he gathered the eggs and placed them in a pan on the kitchen table. Next morning I wanted to show my skill in cooking, but the first egg exploded, leaving a most unpleasant odor. After cleaning up the table, we proceeded with our bacon and eggs breakfast. We had hot biscuits as toast was unheard of in those days.

Charley and I had seven children; Mary Blanche (Mrs. Edward Wright, husband deceased) now living in Laredo, Charles Leslie (wife Dorothy Mainland) of Briscoe Ranch near Catarina, Marguerite Hestel (Mrs. A. D. Campbell) of San Antonio, Paul Park (wife Celia Heye) of Dilley, Texas, Norma (Mrs. Floyd Billings- husband Floyd deceased) of Bruni Texas, William Bernard (wife Bettie Bell Hunter) of Batesville, Texas, Jean Stalling (husband Harold Stalling) of Crystal City, Texas. I now have 29 grandchildren and at present, 34 great grandchildren.

In recalling exciting events, Mom tells the following: Our mother always reminded us, when we went outdoors, to wear our bonnets and to watch out for snakes. When I was six years old, my sister Norma, age 3, and I decided to hunt doodle bugs in a nearby dry creek bed. I was around a bend from my little sister, both of us calling up, "doodle bug, doodle bug come get some clover, when I heard Norma cry out. I ran to her in time to see her shake a small rattlesnake from her hand. It was hanging by its fangs on the underside of her middle finger. The snake dropped off and slithered away under the bank of the creek. I said, "let's go home'" to my crying sister. As we neared the house I told her to hush crying because she would scare our mother. I ran on ahead and as I neared the door I asked my mother to guess what bit Norma. Of course she guessed snake. Then she said, "Oh my God." She proceeded to bind Norma's forearm. She made a poultice of vinegar and soda and put it around the wound and wrapped up my sister's hand. She sent me to my uncle David Park's, a distance of about ¼ mile to get my brother Jay (eight years of age). I ran barefoot all the way and when I saw my brother in the yard playing with my cousin Ora Park, I yelled, "Jay, Mama said come home, a snake bit Norma," and turned back and ran home. Not thinking to inform my Aunt Peggie. It was not until Ora went into the house to ask permission to accompany Jay, that my aunt learned of the snakebite.

My father and other brother George were not at home. They had ridden away early that morning on a cow hunt. In those days there were no fences; people used bells on some of their animals. When they wanted to get up the stock, they had to hunt for them. When my father and George did get home, it was about dark. Immediately George was sent horseback to the Wilsons, three or four miles away, to get saltpeter and whisky thought to be a remedy for snakebite.

By midnight, all the Leona community neighborhood (five or six families), were at our house, each offering a different remedy for rattlesnake bite. Most of the neighbors stayed all night, as Norma was not expected to live. Miraculously, through the mercy of God, Norma lived. She was never able to straighten her finger the rest of her life.

At the time of the snakebite episode, we lived ¼ mile across a dry creek (the big hollow) from Uncle David. Shortly afterwards my father bought a small farm about three miles up the creek and we moved there. Our house had one big room, two shed rooms with the kitchen separated from the house by about four feet. In those days people went to town (Pearsall) about once a month for groceries and the mail. Once after my father had been to town and gotten the month's supply, he and my mother went to the field to harvest some sweet potatoes. While there they looked back and saw that the house was on fire. We children were at school. A neighbor who lived about a mile away came to help salvage our bedroom furniture, but all our clothing except what we were wearing was lost. Our groceries in the kitchen and our kitty Cole, who slept under the kitchen stove, were also lost. This happened in November with cold coming on. We stayed with David Parks, my father's brother, until we could build another house.

Our recreation was dancing. Our neighbor, Mr. Frank Carpenter, usually gave nice dances and suppers on his birthday, July 25th and on Christmas. We either rode horseback or by wagon to the dances. The dances lasted until dawn.

Our religion is Catholic. In the early days there was no church nearer than San Antonio. George and Jay were born in San Antonio, at my grandmother Mudd's home, and were baptized at San Fernando Cathedral. I was baptized in the courthouse in Pearsall. A priest would come from San Antonio and hold mass in private homes. My godparents were Mr. Gabe Hans and a Miss Shelton. Mr. Gabe Hans had a saloon in Pearsall. He had children, Kate and Tom. Tom was a renowned violin player while Kate played the piano. My mother, one of 12 children—all musicians, played the violin and guitar. Her father George W. Mudd was a graduate of the Philadelphia Conservatory of Music in violin. He came from Louisville, Ky. to Somerset, Texas.

I came to the ranch three miles east of Batesville when Charley and I married May 30, 1905. There was only a wagon trail to Pearsall running by our house. In 1912, we bought a house over in Batesville and lived there during the school months in order that Blanche and Leslie start school. In 1920, we bought a house in Uvalde in order that our children could graduate from an accredited high school. In the summer months we always moved back to the ranch. In 1927 we moved back to the ranch, which had always been our permanent home, since 1905. Charley suffered a stroke. He passed away in 1958, but I have continued to live here at the ranch.

A big event in our lives was a trip to the brand new Medina Dam on the occasion of Leslie's birthday, August 18, 1915. We met Norma and Milton and family and occupied tents at the dam. A terrible storm came in the night, blowing down all the tents except ours, and sinking all the boats that were on the lake. We spent the whole next day driving back to our Ranch. The storm had blown down our windmills and caved in our new barn.

In speaking of her father's coming from Scotland she relates:

"Two families immigrated to America from Glasgow, Scotland in about 1850. My father, William Park, born January 12, 1850, was 11 months old at the time they landed on the Texas coast at old Indianola. He was the youngest of four children. During the voyage one parent died and was buried at sea. The other parent died soon after landing at Indianola. A family on the boat took the older two children and probably returned to Scotland. A family named Ridgeway took David and William. All records, logs, were lost when Indianola was washed away by storm and William and David were reared by the Ridgeway family. Nothing is known of the older two children, Archibald and Lillian. It is assumed they were taken back to Scotland. In 1964, when my daughters were in Glasgow, Scotland, they learned that the name Park in Scotland is as common as the name Smith in America. By coincidence, they saw a monument on Lake Lomond dedicated to World War 1 heroes and heading the list was one Archibald Park.

"My father was a ranchman and a participant in one of the last Indian raids in the Loma Vista country in Zavalla County. "Mom faintly remembers the Indian scalp, which she supposed, was burned with their house. These Indians came out of Mexico and would make raids and drive the stock into Mexico. "I think that long black hair and the quiver with arrows must have been burned with our house—I was about 10 years old, I suppose, when the house burned."

"Mrs. Ridgeway's daughter, Aunt Monie, married a Mr. English. They had two children. The people who took Papa and Uncle David had no sons and only the one daughter—when my niece Eva Park McClure lived in San Antonio she had a job as a real estate agent. One of her customers was a Mr. Park whose parents had landed at Indianola the year my father did.

By strange coincidence he had a sister Lillian. By the time Eva wrote me about them she'd lost contact.

"One of Uncle David's sons was named William Archibald and Papa named his son George Archibald after the missing brother. Uncle David was 5 years old when they landed at Indianola. Mrs. Ridgeway said their parents were at least well to do. They had good clothes. Mrs. Ridgeway's supposition was that the Woods soon went back to Scotland. There is a David Park at Devine, a bee man. He came to the ranch once, wanting to buy bees. He may be a descendant. In the last few years I've read of several Park, no "S" in the spelling."

"George and Jay went to school in Pearsall—I suppose, they lived with Uncle Eugene's family. Uncle Eugene and Aunt Sally's daughters were Alice, Gussie, and Eula Henry. Their youngest daughter died at about four years of age. Alice was one of George's favorite cousins."

"A long time ago, before we were married, the Brown, Dunn, Carroll and Carpenter families went on a fishing trip to the Taylor dam on the Nueces River near Carrizo Springs. There was a young couple living in a big house, probably built for tourists when they first developed the irrigation system. A young couple, the William Georges, lived there—called the dam Georges because they lived there and had some connection with irrigation. We asked him about Park families in Scotland. He said there is one under every bush, over there. Since then, Dorothy, Leslie's wife, tells me there are Georges still living around Carrizo Springs. Uncle Milton, a little boy then, got a fishhook clear through his forefinger. Mr. Carpenter and Mr. Dunn cut the hook out. Papa, who was supposed to hold the light, had to quit before he fainted but Milton stood the ordeal—there being no medicine to deaden the pain.

"Lister, our two year old baby brother died of membranous coup, now diptheria. He was the second person buried in the present Pearsall cemetery. The Cox baby was the first. Also, we lost a baby sister who was next older than I—she died immediately after she was born. She was buried in a garden near our house, in the peach orchard. My father probably built her coffin. She was buried across Sandy Creek near Uncle

David's house. Papa had several stands of bees in the garden. Once when Alice Mudd was playing with George, he wishing to show her the, bees took a stick and punched into the beehive. Needless to add Alice saw and felt the bees—all this before I was born. Alice was a pretty girl, probably 15 years old when I was born."

"The place where we crossed the Todos Santos was normally dry. There was a huge grape vine wild there. We used to gather grapes when they were ripe. There was a lake just below the crossing where we could fish. We had a colored lady living with us, Mandy, who loved to go there fishing. This was before my time.

In the early days, roads were terrible. My father was a road overseer. He'd get a crew and they would chop the brush back from the roads. There workers were elected or appointed by it the County Judge. Also, my father was a cattle inspector. I suppose he inspected brands. I still have a little leather bound booklet with a list of cattle brands that were his."

Uncles: World War Two Experiences

Introduction by Edward Wright

I was eight years old when World War II broke out. I definitely remember President Roosevelt's radio address declaring war on December eighth, 1941. It was an anxious time for everyone; for sure it occupied our thoughts for the next four years and changed the world for everyone alive.

Millions of men and women served our country during those years. Some were called on to sacrifice their lives, others were maimed for life. Even those who saw no actual combat were asked to serve at bases in America and other parts of the world. They all contributed. There are as many stories as there were people who served.

I witnessed the anxiety of grandparents, aunts and uncles as they received news of their loved ones in the military. I remember praying for each of them daily during that time. I've long wanted to record the stories of those who were close to me and I asked cousins to pass them on for my grandchildren. These stories were provided by the children and grandchildren of those who served during that war. I still cherish the army shoulder insignia given me by my three uncles.

Charles Leslie Brown, eldest son of Charles and Mary Cecil, was born in Batesville, Texas, August 18, 1908. His wartime experience is recorded by his wife, Dr. Dorothy M. Brown in her book, *The Cowboy and the Unflappable Lady Doctor,* ISBM 09713265-4-1. In it, she recounts that Les volunteered in the army in 1942 at the age of 34. His entire life up till that time was spent in the cattle business in south Texas. He was superintendent of the Briscoe Ranch at the time of enlistment and served in that capacity after the war, until his death on 15 March 1989.

Paul Park Brown

Paul Park Brown, second son of Charles and Mary Cecil was born in Batesville, Texas, 23 April 1913. He married Cecelia Josephine Heye on January 17, 1939, in San Antonio, Texas. Prior to his time in the military, he resided in Laredo and Beeville, Texas, where he was a postal clerk. The couples' daughter, Patricia was born September 11th, 1943.

A 30-year-old married man with child, Paul, was not drafted until later in the war. He was trained as an infantryman and assigned to the 28th division postal section. The division landed in Normandy on July 22nd 1944 and fought from the Normandy hedgerows to the Luxembourg hills. The division was along the Our river by December 16th 1944 when the Battle of the Bulge began. Deeply religious, Paul was 32, ten or more years older than the average GI. He had the rank of Tech Sergeant, but his demeanor, his caring, empathetic personality, made him respected by officers and enlisted in his unit.

Paul's story as he wrote it.

Paul P. Brown

The following is an account of an episode in my life that was not a pleasant one. It also will apply to several thousand other men who suffered the same fate.

It all began in a small city of Luxemburg, not far from the Belgian border, known as Wiltz. My division had been relieved at a position on the German frontier and brought to this place for a rest and to rebuild. We had a front here, considered inactive, using a regiment only to protect the twenty-five miles of difficult terrain. The two remaining regiments were resting and recuperating, preparatory to our next engagement.

I was a member of the postal unit serving the division and also being a part of the division, each member of this unit was a qualified infantryman. But, postal work was our primary duty. Yes, we each had our M-13 and carbines with ammunition.

Being in the rear echelon, however, we were generally from one mile to eight miles from the front. To us, it seemed we were not combat men at all. We only fought, trying with all our power, to get those much looked for and appreciated letters that was so important to the morale of the men on the lines to them. Not bragging, but proud of the fact, we had a group of excellent men under the supervision of a very intelligent captain Billy M. Wall, who worked faithfully to get the mail through. APO28 was the first APO on German soil and considered the most efficient in the ETO.

To get on with my story which includes all members of the rear echelon, the band, Adjutant General's section, Finance section, postal section, Hdqs. Company and the quartermasters section, with the exception of those officers and section chiefs, plus men left behind to take care of removing important records, money etc.

Rumors were flying thick and fast about the German breakthrough that was soon to engulf us all and our positions.

We of the APO had our post office set up in a huge tannery on the fourth floor, accessible by stairs and a freight elevator. Christmas mail was pouring in at the freight elevator at the rate of from five to ten loads each day. It looked very much like a very happy Christmas was in store for all the men of our division. A huge amount of mail was broken down awaiting delivery to the various regiments and units.

In spite of the above-mentioned rumors, even though they were confirmed by our reconnaissance patrol, we felt secure and sure that the Germans would never be successful in any breakthrough. We were soon to be mistaken.

On the night of Saturday, December 16, 1944, after we were all in bed, our captain came down and woke us. We all had to roll our packs and be prepared to fall out at a moment's notice. Nothing else happened and we all went back to bed, thinking it a dry run or false alarm.

Sunday morning at about ten o'clock word came to fall out, preparatory to going up to designated positions. From all we could gather, both officers and men thought it still just a dry run. Some of the boys did not even bother to put on their heavy clothes necessary in this cold climate.

We marched to our respective platoon positions, dug in and made ourselves as comfortable as possible in a wooded area approximately a mile east of Wiltz. We had our k-rations about dark.

At about twelve o'clock that night a jeep came by with some officers in it. They told us the Germans had been halted and that in an hour we would be going back in for a good night's rest.

At about two in the morning, word came for our platoon to move out to another position. We then took a road that led to the outskirts of Wiltz. We turned off and took the road that let to Clervaux. We followed this until we came to a barn, where we remained the balance of the night; bedding down in nice clean straw.

At daylight, we were given a hot cup of coffee and then we marched on down the Clervaux road. We passed the defense platoon, dug in on the side of a hill. As we passed them, shouts could be heard, telling the defense platoon, Not to Worry, we were going to take on the Jerries. A lot of laughing and ridiculing went on as we passed them.

We were led by a second lieutenant Smith, a very likeable man and affectionately known as "Smitty" to all the men. After marching some three miles down the road we came upon a unit of the 639th TD battalion and our purpose was to give this unit support. Their officers and noncommissioned took men of my squad and placed them at various points overlooking surrounding ravines and hills. The country was very rugged.

A private named Pocarp and myself were taken up to the foremost gun position down the road. We were told they had enough men there so we retraced our steps for a hundred yards or so and settled in a two man foxhole at the edge of the road that the retreating Germans had so conveniently dug in their retreat two months before.

From this position, we overlooked a deep ravine and could watch the road where it soon doubled back behind the opposite hill, went out of sight behind the hill and came into view a mile or so beyond again, where the country was almost a plateau.

After scanning the farthest part of the road for a while, suddenly it seemed alive with troops. A few minutes later, two Luxemburg girls came running up the road crying, "The Germans come." their faces pale as death. I sent Pocarp up to the command post to report what we had observed. On his return, I sent him down to the gun position to report. He came back with another boy and some field glasses. We studied the troops and the road for some time. Shortly we looked just across the ravine on the point where the road disappeared behind the hill and to our surprise, the Jerries were setting up a machine gun.

The boy who had the field glasses shot the shot that started the fireworks. He sent a token shot with his carbine. I feel that he did no damage, as the distance was approximately six hundred yards. At any rate, hell really broke loose and the Germans soon disappeared behind the hill after spraying our foxhole a bit with machine gun fire. For some unknown reason, all that excitement seemed fun.

Pvt. Pocarp got worried and wanted to get out of there quick. He had reasons for his fears, as in front of us was the deep, ravine and the Germans, behind us a cliff formed when the road was cut out of the hill. Our only escape was up the road, which was very straight, parallel to the hill the Germans had. I chided him, saying we were alright and would leave in due course. I was intent in holding this position as long as our guns were still below us. They had two tank destroyers and an M-18 Recon car.

The Germans, after our first barrage of fire, simply withdrew and came over the hill below us and started their drive straight up the ravine towards us flanking us on both sides.

When the going got tough, the men below us destroyed their gun and moved out in the tank destroyer and the recon car. When they first came by I tried to hail them, to no avail. None stopped and I wished I had listened to Pocarp, as we had to get out the best we could.

I let him go first, instructing him to use his basic training of hitting the ground, crawling and getting up and running. Repeating this until he had traversed the four hundred yards of straight road that had no foliage or bank to give us much protection from enemy fire.

He left and after an interval I followed. It was no easy job, considering we had on overshoes, overcoat covered with a raincoat, rifle and ammo. Pocarp made it and I was on my last run when I glanced down to see tracer fire bouncing off the pavement at my feet. Without further inducement I dived into the ravine, only to find myself in still a very bad position. Corporal MCDonold, Jack Kennet and Pat Welch were on a machine gun firing directly over me and to suddenly appear in front of them would be dangerous indeed, considering the strain we were in. My faithful friend Pocarp came to my rescue by getting to them and letting them know where I was. They let me out and I promptly got over the hill out of range to get my breath again and get control of myself.

I then had the boys on the hill withdraw to the top of the hill, realizing they would soon be pinned down on the slope as soon as the Jerries located them. Shortly after, the Germans had us located and began throwing mortar fire at us. The lieutenant decided to withdraw, destroying two more of his guns. I tried to locate my squad, but they had been scattered around so much I didn't know where they all were. I found all I could and told them what was happening, started to get the boys on the machinegun. A mortar shell landed close by and before I got to their position I met them coming. They destroyed the machine gun after using up all their ammo. We loaded on the halftracks and pulled out, setting up in a small village a mile or so down the road. In an hour or so Lt. Smith and the other officers whom I couldn't find, joined us there after several narrow escapes.

We dispersed here and held for several hours until the 44th engineer battalion came up. The Germans seemed to be everywhere and it was difficult to tell which troops were ours. From here and before nightfall, my squad, which was attached to the 630th, withdrew with them back to the outskirts of Wiltz, where we took over houses for defense purposes and sat the guns up in the streets. Here we remained throughout the night and next day. We tried to rest between watches, but that was hard to do. C-rations were brought in, the first food we had since the night before, but no one was especially hungry.

All that night and the next day we were on guard, keeping the Germans from crossing a river and flanking us. We'd eat a K-ration the next day.

Our platoons were separated and no communications seemed to exist. To us, who were being baptized to actual front line duties, everything was in a terrible mess. I think that same feeling applied to the officers as well. We watched seven tanks maneuver on a patch of woods and fire several rounds into them only to see them withdraw shortly. Later, we were told, the 44th engineers had been in there instead of the Germans. If this was true, then you can imagine the confusion that existed at that time.

We were told late in the afternoon that the town was completely surrounded and when night fell we were to get out the best way we could. The town was to be surrendered.

At about 8:30, which was dark there, the bridge was blown, to delay German entry into town. We loaded on half-tracks and moved out. The tracks were loaded with men. I'm not one to question military strategy, but I can't understand why the seven or nine tanks in the town, plus the half-tracks and all the available men were not used all together to spearhead our way through enemy lines that had us surrounded. I believe we could have gone all the way through to Bastogne.

111

As it happened, we in the tracks pulled out. Some ten miles out of Wiltz at the first road intersection, we were stopped by Belgians of the resistance movement and told that at the next crossroad where the road to Bastogne forked, the Germans had a roadblock. We stopped there and a jeep was dispatched back to Wiltz for instructions. It never returned, nor did my friend Mc Donald who went along as a guide. The Germans were letting troops out of Wiltz but not in.

We dispersed in the woods to await further orders. While there, four Germans came marching down the road in perfect cadence. They were challenged by our sentries and after a pause, tried to shoot, but it wound up with one dead German and three escapees.

Later three half-tracks came upon us and thinking we were the Germans, switched on their lights and opened up on us with 50 caliber machine guns. They were finally stopped and told us they were going to run that roadblock and all who wanted to risk it pile in the tracks. I guess everyone did as the tracks were sure packed.

We came to the roadblock shortly and the Germans met us with firepower. The drivers suddenly turned on the lights again and opened up. We went through the roadblocks without losing a vehicle and very few casualties. Don't think the Germans can say that.

Since we were unable to turn right at that roadblock, we took the next road to the right. This took us to a small village, apparently unoccupied by the Germans. We stopped there for directions. A Belgian priest and some sisters were just going into the rectory. The small priest came out. He tried to give us directions, saying he thought the road was still open. Due to the language difficulty, he elected to go with us with the understanding we would bring him back, which was agreeable. A jeep came to the front of the convoy and it was full, the small priest got on the right front fender and we pulled out. We were not far out when we came upon some GI's, apparently wounded, crying for us to stop. It may or may not have been a GI. Anyway, they yelled to him. We would send an ambulance back. I think it was a German hoax, only to stop the convoy.

Farther on at a place where the road was cut around a hill, we met a heavy concentrated amount of fire. It seemed the whole hill was exploding. We turned on our lights again and a wagon loaded was crossways in the road. Then suddenly there was a terrific explosion and the halftrack came to a sudden halt. The terrible cries of our wounded were awful. It seemed we were all doomed. What happened I don't know, for I was stunned for a bit. I only had a flesh would across my hip so far. We were all just waiting for that fatal sting of hot lead. Suddenly, all was quiet and the Germans were everywhere. Slowly it dawned on us that we were captured, like rats in a trap. We were German prisoners. What an awful feeling, when that realization struck us. The wounded and dead, the agonies of the dying, it's something no mortal can describe. How many, I don't know. I do know of the men of the APO. Jack Kennett's legs were almost blown off, Charles Rube was shot mighty bad in his right arm. Paul Palmer, shot through the leg, a flesh wound, Tommie Jender lost his good eye and I got the above mentioned flesh wound.

We were prisoners of war in the hands of the Germans, and those of us who could were slowly climbing off the tracks with our hands high above our heads. We were now at their mercy and were wondering what would happen next. We had been told the Germans were taking no prisoners.

As each of us dismounted, a German was there to search us. Even the serious wounded had to have their hands up. Charles was shot very badly in his right arm and he was forced to keep his hands up. There seemed to be no medical aid and when we tried to help the wounded we were shoved along with no heed to our request, as were the wounded that could walk. Later the wounded were taken away and some did get medical aid of some sort. Jack Kennett was the first person I heard when our track was blown up. He was begging for the shooting to stop. He was mortally wounded in the leg from what I could gather. How serious I did not know, but have since learned that he was killed in action in the bulge, so I presume he died of that wound. How long he lived I do not know.

As we were searched, the first thing taken from me was my watch. Several Germans searched us, each taking what the other had missed. They took my watch, fountain pen, knife, flashlight, cigarettes and a box of k-rations. One took my pocket book, but I heard the boy in front of me say when they took his, that it had his prayer book and it was given back.

I said the same thing and mine was returned. That pocket book did have my prayer book, also the pictures of my wife and pictures of my baby at her first birthday and were my most prized possessions. I got to keep them throughout. All this was happening at night. When they took my knife I sure thought my last hour was at hand. The Jerry took it and after looking at it, shook his head as if to say "It's too bad you had this.

He gave me a shove up the road into the blackness and it looked like I was alone. It was a very trying moment, until I came upon some more of my buddies. We were moved up the road for a little way and then turned off into a sort of an amphitheater, formed by the hills joining. Here another German grabbed me and took my overcoat. It turned out he wanted it for one of my wounded buddies, who had on a mackinaw. I was given the mackinaw. I was thankful for the trade later, as I found eight cigarettes in the pockets. The Jerries had taken all mine. We were put in rows up the side of the hill and our position still looked very grave, what with the guard all around us, carrying all sorts of guns. We still thought the Jerries intended killing us all. It is my firm conviction that was their intentions only they had captured so many of us they couldn't afford to. That did happen at Malmady, I've since learned.

We were kept on this hill all night. It was miserably cold, but we still had on our overshoes and kept close together, straddling one another and getting our bodies as close as possible. Some, if not all of us got a little sleep this way. At about daylight they moved us out. As we got on the road there was a pile of Americans bodies stacked in cordwood fashion and covered with a GI blanket, how many, I don't know. As we moved on up the road dead were everywhere, both German and American. One American was still alive begging for water even though he was partly covered by snow. A lot of the dead were almost completely covered. It had been a bloody night indeed and we who were still alive considered ourselves very lucky and reverently thanked the good Lord.

We were marched about two miles and put in a barn for the day. We were very hungry, but getting anything to eat was another matter. We found some raw cabbage leaves we found in that barn. Someone stole a loaf of bread from the Germans, only a couple or three shared it however. Late that evening we were moved to another large barn at a road intersection one kilometer from a village of Syr. This must have been in Belgium. We saw a lot of our wounded there, but only recognized a few. We spent a miserable night with very little straw and no cover. We kept warm by sleeping so crowded.

The next morning we were called out and had to do a bit of cleaning up of debris around the building. Our fingers were nearly frozen, as we had no gloves. They had taken our gloves the night before while searching us. Then we were lined up and it was then when I realized how many Americans they had captured that night. Must have been around eight hundred in all. They still had given us no food and the hunger pains were getting terrific. Guards were everywhere. We started a march then, toward Germany and that march continued until about one o'clock the following morning. Some estimated it at about 57 kilometers or around 35 miles. The guard in charge carried a luger pistol constantly in his hands. Occasionally, we were permitted to stop for a rest. Once we stopped by a Luxembourger's garden and managed to get some raw cabbage and Brussels sprouts, which really tasted good. The guards also let the boys who still had helmets go to a small creek beyond the garden and bring back some drinking water. Most of us had our helmets taken from us where they captured us. We were bareheaded; some had blankets over their heads to keep warm. Prior to that river, we had been eating snow when we were thirsty. All this country was very rough and mountainous. We were fortunate in that the road we were on was paved. We were constantly meeting German soldiers going up to the front. Most all their equipment was being hauled in wagons, some huge trucks would go lumbering by either pulling guns or else would be towing a couple of army cars. It seemed they all lacked sufficient gasoline. All were well camouflaged and as they went by us the gas fumes from the vehicles were almost stifling. It must have been a very cheap grade of gasoline. Some were operated by burners, either coal or wood. We kept heading toward Germany.

As the day passed on, more and more of the weaker boys began falling out. Later they were put on passing vehicles and brought up to the column. That march continued on way after night until almost one in the morning. We finally came to a village high upon a mountain where we halted. While waiting there, almost dead from the long march and steady climb, a group of tiger tanks passed by. They only traveled after dark I suppose.

We were finally put in a barn with no food, but all were so exhausted we went to sleep. It was so crowded finding room to stretch out was impossibility, but we slept.

The next morning we were moved to another town some three or four miles and placed in another barn, just as crowded. That evening a barrel of Sauer kraut, uncooked was set in the door. The men were so starved, that lots of the men never got a thing. I managed to get two hands full of the stuff. Our stomachs were so empty I was afraid to eat much of it. That day several men were called out to butcher some hogs, presumably to feed us with. These were taken from the Luxembourgers.

We all knew we would at last get something the next morning to eat so all went to sleep with high hopes. The next morning they began letting us out of the barn a few at a time. They had cooked some sauerkraut, boiled some potatoes and put out some salt. There was no meat. A few got bone to nibble on. We had nothing to eat out of. As each would dig in with both hands and get all he could and move on. That bit of nourishment surely helped a lot. We couldn't have gone much further without it. We spent another night in that barn. Davey Follweiler and I were together through this, he having a blanket, we managed to sleep a bit warmer by keeping close to one another.

The next morning we were called out and lined up in columns of five, and were passed out a loaf of bread for five men and about 4 oz. of sausages which was to be our rations for the next two days.

An incident happened the day before we arrived at the above-mentioned barn—we were lined up and German soldiers came through the men checking our shoes and overshoes. One found me and placing his foot by mine, made me give him my overshoes. I could have killed him had it been possible as snow was about a foot deep and my shoes were about worn out, but I had to give them up. Some even took the boys shoes and gave them theirs which were worn out. To my notion, that was the worst thing they had done so far. That was an arrogant group of young Germans there and I suppose they then actually believed they were the super race. I saw one German soldier deliberately kick one of our officers because he was on the wrong side of the road. Our march continued after the Germans had gotten themselves all fitted out with our shoes.

After we had our rations we moved on, our destination being Bitburg, Germany. How far we marched that day, I don't know. We arrived at Bitburg at about midnight and it was burning. Our planes had been there in the afternoon. The city was in an awful mess and getting through the streets was an ordeal. Before we arrived some seven of eight miles out, I developed a terrible pain in my right groin, so intense I wanted to fall out and take whatever consequences the Jerries would deal out, but my buddies Dave Echles and Robbins wouldn't hear of that. They took turns in partly carrying me. We could see the red glow of the fires and knew we had not much further to go.

By the time we arrived, my pains had left me and I felt lots better. I still feel I owe these friends of mine, the above and one other, who had been with us in the APO, a lot, as I'd never have arrived in Bitburg had it not been for their kindness.

When we arrived in Bitburg, other Americans who had arrived before us were working to clean the streets. Our group was halted and told to get busy. We were all too completely exhausted to do any work. The guards would go to the head of our column and get those started. We of the rear would sit down. Then here they would come and force us to work. Those in front would stop. Guess the Germans soon gave up as we marched a ways across town, arriving in a group of barracks in a fork of the incoming roads to the town. We stood around outside until almost four in the morning. Snow covered the ground and we had no shelter, so had to keep moving for fear of freezing. The barracks were full of the Americans, preceding us.

At about four in the morning, the Germans moved that group out and we took over their barracks. They had fires and the buildings were nice and warm. We found beds and mattresses, got warm and really slept. This was the first time we were actually warm since our capture.

That was Christmas Eve when we arrived in Bitburg—and a sad one it was.

That morning, Christmas day, at about nine, we were awakened by the drone of airplanes. Some went out to see them. I was on the top of a three-tier bunk when I heard the bombs released. That was the first time I ever heard them, but I knew what they were and promptly rolled off that bunk and under it just as the bombs began falling. They fell very close, tearing up some of the barracks. Rock and debris came through the roof, injuring a boy next to me.

How many were hurt and killed I don't know. The road intersection was completely knocked out. We got outside and rushed for some covered trenches further from the crossroads before the bombers came back. They did return twice and let go while we in those trenches fervently praying they wouldn't land on us. It was a terrible ordeal. Watching another group of planes approaching, we saw a big B-17 bomber explode in the air. German flak had made a direct hit. Only three parachutes came floating down. Later two of the fliers joined us. The Jerries had picked them up. I don't know what happened to the third. Our guards had all ran some three hundred yards to an open field. They were mortally afraid of our planes. When all was quiet again, ambulances and trucks carried away the dead and wounded.

I wonder how many of our men were killed there! We spent the rest of the day with the Germans trying to make us clean the streets to no avail. This was Christmas day for us. That night we spent in what was left of our barracks. We managed to sing Christmas Carrols in spite of our hunger and predicament.

The next day we were marched out to a hill covered with forest. The Germans evidently expected the planes back. No bombers returned, however, our fighters did, and we had a ringside seat watching them dive and knock the Flack Field that was responsible for knocking out our bomber the day before. That evening we were fed a bowl of potato soup. I was given a thick slice of bread by Captain McLeod, personnel officer of our 109th infantry regiment, as we watched from that hillside.

The next morning, Dec. 27, we were called out to begin our march once more. We were given another bowl of potato soup. Some managed to get two bowls. We were beginning to realize we had to outwit the Germans every chance for extra food if we were to survive.

Here, Dave and I were separated from Echles and Robbins. They were in a group that took some other route. Joe Praissler was with us, and another boy from the APO. That was another long march that took us into Wittlich, Germany. We arrived there after dark. There was a real prison with several stories, catwalks and very similar to our prisons in the states. Planes had worked the city over that day. It seemed our planes worked just ahead of us. We were put in a large room, some two hundred of us. The heavy doors were locked. We had mats to lie on.

The water system had been destroyed. When we wanted to go to the latrines we had to rap on the door to be let out. There were toilets but no water and these were soon filthy and the stench was horrible. Details were called out, sixteen men at a time, to pump water with a double action hand pump that took eight men at a time to operate. We had to supply water for a kitchen that made soup for part of the civilians. It was bitter cold and our hands almost froze. The kitchen was operated by slave labor and one was in charge of the pump. We soon got on his good side and he smuggled us a large can of thick barley soup, which we ate on as we pumped water. The men inside were served a little bit of this, not nearly so much as we on the pumps. We ate all we could and filled our supplies containers we had picked up on the road to eat out of. This extra we carried to our buddies who could not get out.

The following day I was placed on a detail to do some cleanup work. We had still not been registered as prisoners of war and had to do what the Germans wanted or else suffer. This day, Dave and I were together with six more guys. We were marched into the town by guards and turned over to a very mean looking German civilian. He cursed us and raised hell all in German language, for as long as the Germans were in sight. Then he got quiet. We didn't know what to expect from him. He took us down to a house that had been partly demolished by our bombs and told us by signs to start carrying the boards across the street and clearing the debris. We piddled, simulating work. Our hands were too cold to do anything. I got up on what had been the second story and evidently a kitchen. I would pick up pictures and toss them down to this civilian. Frozen apples were scattered everywhere, so being hungry, I ate those on the sly until I was pretty full on them. I decided to ask the guy there if it were all right if I ate them. I held one up and made the necessary signs. He nodded his head in approval. After a while he put a couple of the boys to cleaning out the cellar. He called me down from my second story perch after a little and motioned all of us over to a bag full of apples the boys had brought from the cellar. So, again we helped ourselves to all the apples we wanted and stuffed our pockets full. I'll call the old bird a gentleman now. He never gave us another order. We did simulate work until about twelve-thirty when a lady comes up with a big covered kettle. It was full of pea soup without the soup and surely tasted good. She brought out a loaf of hard bread that was partly full of dust from the explosion and a good bread knife. We really filed up but were so full of apples we couldn't eat it all. So we got cans and took the remaining stuff. The lady asked if any one of us were from Pennsylvania.

Dave said he was. The lady then asked if he were near Erie and he said no. He could talk a little of what he called Pennsylvania Dutch so could understand her a little. It turned out she had a sister living in Erie.

After our meal we were marched back to our prison, feeling we had been very fortunate in our detail. We shared our apples and soup with our buddies again. A lot of other details were put to digging graves and had no food. Yes we were lucky; we went in with a full stomach.

The next day, four of us who were buddies—Dave Praissler, another boy and myself—were put on another detail, which took us to a hospital. A rather large one, two long parallel four-story buildings with a large red cross painted in the parade ground between the buildings. We put to work cleaning out some rooms and putting up beds. We worked until about noon and then asked for some food. They called us into a room where three Germans were and gave us a large bowl of soup and some bread. We really feasted again if one can call soup a feast. It was to us. Anyway, as soup won't stay with one very long, one of the Germans was a big strapping fellow who knew all the American song hits, and he would sing them for us. He talked some English. He was not over twenty-two. We talked some to him, or rather he to us. One of the things he told us was rather amazing. He said, "You know, it is really a shame for us to have to be trying to kill one another. I have nothing against you, nor you I. It's because of our leaders, Hitler (he mentioned Hitler first), Stalin, Churchill and Roosevelt, that we are fighting one another." He continued, "I like America and Americans and if the United States ever lets any Germans come there again after this war, I'm coming over there to make my home, no more of this Germany for me."

That really floored us. Here was a German, evidently one of Hitler's youth, talking in this manner. Of course we told him what a wonderful land ours was. We left with the impression that here was one German youth who knew Germany was licked and had some sense.

There was a Bringe, (railroad) rather close by. That afternoon the sirens turned loose, signifying planes were in the immediate vicinity. We were still on the fourth floor when we heard the swish of bombs falling; everyone tore down the stairs to the basement. The first bomb landed almost dead center in the huge Red Cross in the parade grounds. They only made the one run. Afterwards, the Germans had us carrying patients to the basements. We did this for a while with one German beating us on the backs cursing us because it was our planes. After a little, another came for us. We followed him down the long hallway. He opened a door and there lay a bomb that hadn't gone off. He gave us a stretcher to put the bomb on. We protested until he went for his "mercy pistol" which all German medics seemed to carry. It was either remove the bomb or get shot. I told the boys I'd rather remove the bomb. If it goes off, well we'll never know it anyway. After a prayer, we tackled it. The Germans took off. Handling it with extreme care, we got it on a stretcher. It must have weighed about two hundred or so pounds. We carried it a couple or three hundred yards into a field and put it into a bomb crater made in the same raid. We breathed a sigh of relief when we had gotten away from it. We were soon discouraged again though as we were escorted into the opposite building, a door was opened and there was another. Would the good Lord be with us again was the question in our minds. This bomb had also come through to the ground floor, had hit sideways and bounced, wedging itself in a door with its nose some eight or ten inches from the floor. This was so much worse than the first. We found some wire and fastener in the hole; I suppose to hold them in the bomb racks. With the greatest of caution the four of us gradually worked it loose from the door panel and laid it on the stretcher. We carried it to another bomb crater successfully. Thank God that was the last. We all felt the Good Lord was with us and since neither had gone off we could take anything the Germans would deal out to us short of actual murder. Those were dreadful moments of our lives. We carried a few more patients then and our guard came for us. We were given a can of some sort of meat to eat and then taken back to the prison in Wittlich. A day had passed that we shall never forget.

Paul never finished writing his story. His son, Charles, said it was too painful to continue. By Christmas, 1945, Paul had been freed and was back home rehabilitating. He shared some of his story with me, an impressionable twelve year old. As Charles grew up, Paul shared the story with him. Here is the rest of the story as best we understand.

From Wittlich the prisoner's march continued till they reached Stalag 13B near Weiden, and from there they were herded into railroad cars - crammed with little room to lie down. They traveled east for several days, halting as higher priority traffic passed. They were fed intermittently, and huddled together for warmth in the freezing January weather, finally arriving in Stallag 4B near Muhlberg, Germany. The family received a letter from him there on February 2, 1945; ending several months of anxiety.

As the war wore down, the Russian Army approached Muhlberg and the prisoners were forced to march north and West in a line including civilian refugees. They were constantly harassed by Allied bombers over the next 60 days of walking. Disease including Diphtheria and frequent diarrhea became so common that finally a field hospital was set up by the road near Brunswick, Germany. Many of the prisoners died; all of them lost significant weight. Paul estimated he could have survived another ten days before expiring, but he volunteered to help in the hospital.

On April 12th 1945 the American 30th Division broke through the lines and began to evacuate the severely depleted patients in the hospital. Doctors were forced to decide which ones of the most critical patients were to be taken first and which left to possible death. One of Paul's friends who was in a coma was left out as too far gone to be prioritized for transportation. Paul stopped an ambulance by standing in front of it and convinced the driver to take his friend. He remembered that incident and was able to contact that friend to renew their relationship thirty years later.

A shadow of his former self, Paul was hospitalized as were the rest of the men in that hospital. He finally made it back to Texas and his anxious family.

He returned to work in the post office, this time moving his family to property west of Dilley, Texas—where he lived the rest of his life. Paul and Celie had six more children after he was freed.

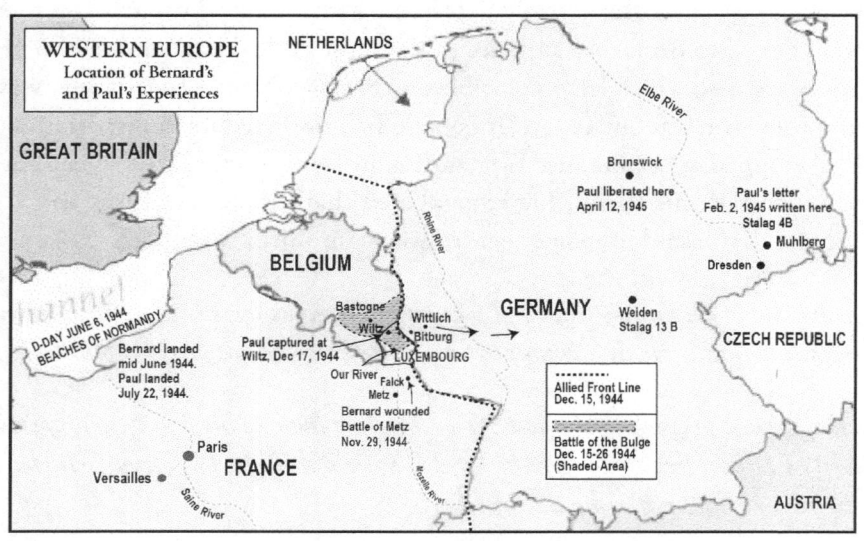

Western Europe: Location of Bernard's and Paul's Experiences

Bernard & Bette Belle Brown

Bernard's Story

By Edward Wright

William Bernard Brown, born in Uvalde, Texas on 10/10/1921 was the nearest thing to an older brother I had. Eleven years younger, I followed his example of what life's steps should be during my teens and early twenties. He taught me what friends were in his relationship with John William Maddox, and with Pinky Brown (no kin); he taught me to swim in the Leona River – after stacking maize to dry in the field all day. He taught me to hunt, even though I put a bullet through his roof. Following his example, I enrolled at Texas A&M and in ROTC, then later received a commission as a 2nd lieutenant.

I recall the anxiety the Brown family felt during World War Two as my mother's three brothers either volunteered or were drafted into the army. That anxiety peaked in the fall of 1944 when news of Bernard's wounding and Paul's disappearance and capture arrived in the mail. They both survived, and were back in Texas by Christmas, 1945. Paul acquired the family property in Frio County my great grandfather had farmed, and determined to move his family as soon as possible. My Dad and others volunteered to help update the house. Twelve years old, I got to tag along, and during breaks, I got to listen to Paul and Bernard tell the story of their hard year, just passed. Bernard, still recuperating from his broken hip, was not able to do much work so I heard more of his experience. This is what I heard then and during hunting weekends in the following years.

When World War Two broke out Bernard was a sophomore in the Corps of Cadets at A&M and as such was protected from the draft. He and Senorita – Bette-Belle - married over the Christmas holidays in 1942. His deferred status lasted until April, 1943 when most of his class was drafted and commissioned as Second Lieutenants in the army. He was not graduated. Bernard was sent to the infantry school in Fort Benning, Georgia. I'm unsure what additional training he received, but he arrived in Normandy in June of 1944, weeks after D Day. Assigned to the 95th Infantry Division, he volunteered for night duty as a scout behind enemy lines. The unit advanced through France over the next 5 months. I know of no incidents Bernard related for this period.

November found the outfit in the area of the Moselle River in Northern France, near Metz. On November 29th, Bernard, a platoon leader, and his unit were ordered to do a daytime raid. A German Artillery piece deployed on a nearby hill above his unit was the target. Advancing up the hill in a forest of trees, the unit saw no one. Bernard walked by a tree and found himself face to face with a German who seemed equally surprised to see him. I recall him saying the distance was less than fifty yards. The German raised his weapon and Bernard's reaction was to duck behind the tree he'd just passed. He got most of his body in except his right leg. Two bullets from the 'burp' gun struck him. One hit the field glasses dangling from his neck, probably saving his life; the other struck his right leg and hit his thigh bone, creating a compound fracture. He went down when his leg gave way, and passed out.

The next thing he remembered was waking when he was being searched by a German soldier who took personal effects and a German Luger pistol Bernard had picked up somewhere along the way. Bernard recalled passing out either from shock or pain several times but awoke later with two soldiers pointing rifles at him. At this point, a German officer walked up, looked down at his lieutenant's bars and pointing at his own rank insignia he said, "Uberlutnant"; pointing at Bernard he said "Unterlutnant," indicating he was superior to him in rank. To Bernard's surprise, a German medic, Bernard described him as a small man, was ordered to look at his wounds. Whether or not he was ordered, or if the medic did it on his own, he instructed the two soldiers to fabricate a litter and carry Bernard to a group of houses on a hillside. These houses may have been caves or mines with the entrance walled over. In any case, they were equipped with a basement and the medic went with him down steps to a cellar like area where French civilians were huddled. Apparently the two soldiers left. The medic tended to Bernard as best he could. Bernard remembered him asking if Bernard could get him to the United States. I'm not sure what Bernard replied. I'm uncertain how long Bernard was in that basement but he drifted in and out of consciousness.

At least one, perhaps two or more days, passed before the area was being occupied by British troops who were clearing the vicinity of Germans. Their custom was to call out for anyone inside each structure to surrender. If no one came out, they threw a grenade to assure the area was safe. Fortunately, when they came to the basement Bernard was in he was awake and was able to shout, "Don't shoot; there's an American in here!" or some such yell.

And so he was evacuated to a field hospital, then to a major facility in France. He was air-evacuated to a hospital in England for the first of many surgeries. I believe he was brought back to hospitals in the US by ship, first to the Northeast, but later to Fort Bliss in El Paso, where he had numerous surgeries to repair his thigh. When I listened to him that

Christmas he was between surgeries; he was to endure many more. Finally fitted to special boots, he endured having one leg shorter than the other for the rest of his life.

For participating in the attack up that hill, Bernard received the Silver Star, and of course the Purple Heart award. He never found out what happened to the medic.

Bernard went on through the rest of his life as a productive rancher, citizen and neighbor in Zavalla County. He was generous to all he met. He and Betty Belle raised three children to maturity, though they lost 6-year old Susan to cancer. He died June 21, 1996.

Grandma, Bill, Les

Wartime Letters from Les Brown to His Parents, Charles and Mary Cecil Brown

Transcribed by Elizabeth Alexander, comments by Edward Wright

Separated from home and friends during World War Two, letters to and from home were a connection to all that was familiar. Fortunately, Les' mother kept them for posterity and his daughter, Elizabeth, transcribed them. They say a lot about Les and the times in which he was living.

Born August 18, 1908, Charles Leslie Brown was 32 years old when World War two broke out. Single, dedicated to his life as a rancher, faced with eventual call up for the draft, 33 year old Les volunteered for the Army Air Corps and was inducted at Fort Sam Houston in San Antonio on July 2nd, 1942. Coincidentally, his first cousin, Vincent Brown enlisted at the same time. A letter July 6, shows Les still waiting for indoctrination, not uncommon in the massive call up of manpower.

His next letter, four days later, shows him at Sheppard Field in Wichita Falls, TX, the Air Corps replacement center, wondering where he will be placed. He is to go through basic training there.

He ended up at Lowry Field, Denver, CO—at armament school for August and September 1942. He had been selected for training on the top secret Nordon bombsight. Thirty were picked out of 400 considered.

Throughout his letters home, he tells of mail he received from friends or relatives, he comments that insurance on his car—eventually left with his younger sister, Hestel—is still active. He is especially interested of the comings and goings of the Briscoe family and the ranch, where he had worked since 1939.

By his October 3rd letter he tells of graduating from the bombsight maintenance school, and is headed to Geiger Field, Washington State. He was able to stop at the Great Salt Lake and then visit Yellowstone Park on the way north.

From Geiger Field he reports he's been eating well, exercising, and has gained weight. Of obvious interest to him is that Dolph Briscoe, Sr., his employer, friend and benefactor, wrote that the military intends to take over thirteen thousand acres of their beloved Briscoe ranch for a gunnery and bombing range.

December 7th, a year after Pearl Harbor, he is assigned to Ephrata Field, Washington. Dolph Jr.'s marriage keeps his thoughts on home.

A few days later, December 12, 1942, he comments to his parents on his brother Paul's call up to the military; and Paul's tough move from Beeville to San Antonio. Paul felt he would be gone for a while and call up entails closing up his home for the move. Les further comments that the boys in the military have it easy, with food and gasoline rationing hitting civilians hard.

Ten-day Christmas leaves are available for him, but since the only transportation available is railroads with priority given to military necessity travel, he'd only get home in time to return.

By January, six months after enlistment, Les is made corporal. Reporting another contact from home, he tells of a letter from niece, seven year old Mary Paul, telling about the whooping cough in the family. He remains in Ephrata, Washington, assigned to the 359th bomb squadron.

As ever, keeping close touch with the Briscoes, he includes a letter from Dolph telling he'd shipped 100 of Les's steers north to be fattened. (Apparently, while he was gone, Briscoe managed his ranching investments.) Les comments that he has applied for deferment of income tax, which was a wartime benefit.

By March 1943 he's assigned to the army air base at Moses Lake, Washington—63rd Air Operations Squadron. He commented on the birth of Bill Billings, new son of his sister Norma, and the death of his cousin, (first cousin once removed and also uncle) Frank Brown—also, Les repeatedly invests his earnings from various sources or investments into US War Bonds. Single, with savings collected over the years, he unselfishly asks his parents to make his funds available to siblings Bernard, Hestel, Paul. He worries that if Hestel buys his car she won't be able to get tires.

In April he's able to visit the new Grand Coulee Dam in Washington.

Enlisted for less than a year, Les is now a sergeant, living in a tent and eating K-rations. Apparently housing has not caught up to the Moses Lake Field. He is hearing rumors of overseas moves. Still reflecting on

131

back home, he comments on the rains in south Texas, his father's bees, his mother's canning and is thankful to Jeanne for sending cookies.

Apparently, there is much need for his bombsight services as flying is a constant thing at his base. Rumors of overseas assignment abound.

Busy as they were, they were still having gas mask training for everyone. No one had used gas during the war, but in 1942 the government was still concerned.

Les is still emotionally tied to the ranch and old friends; Ariel Shearer is a frequent correspondent. Les has apparently become a bombardier, not just a bombsight maintenance man, as he is now required to fly for 20 hours per month.

In September 1943 he was given a 14-day furlough, and spent eight of those days traveling. On his way back he spent the night with the Heyes, Paul's in-laws in San Antonio.

Paul arrived on furlough only a few days after Les passed through. He wrote in a letter to Jeanne, "Tell Mom and Papa not to feed all the chickens to Les. I know it's first come first serve, but I' going to be hungry too." He didn't know how prophetic that statement would be!

Paul had become a Papa, as Patricia was born.

In November, from letters, Les assumes that Paul has been shipped overseas. Les has been told his unit is going overseas as well.

The sergeants in his unit volunteered for KP to give the privates an opportunity to enjoy Thanksgiving dinner, and his CO suggested they volunteer for KP on the ship going overseas, as they would get first choice for the food. Still connected to family, Les hails youngest brother Bernard's commission in the army, and comments on Bernard and Betty-Belle's marriage discussions.

He next reports from a demarcation point in San Francisco, he points out that censors would cut out anything about the when or where of his departure. By the end of December they are on a ship bound for Hawaii and the next letter talks of swimming in the ocean most afternoons. No beach is mentioned. His letters are coming via V-mail.

For the next six months, letters from home are the biggest topic of his comments; he keeps track of Bernard and Paul, Pop and his honeybees. Entertainment is playing softball, watching rodeos, and seeing comedians like Bob Hope and Jack Benny. His whole outfit lined up along the road for a glimpse of FDR. They stood for three hours to see him drive by. He tells his folks that mail was frozen till Roosevelt left the island, but Japanese propaganda radio, Tokio Rose, talked about it while he was there.

His November 7th 1944 letter tells of being transferred by air to Kauai. Four months after the D-day invasion he comments on the battle in Europe going our way as well as in the Pacific. Brothers Paul and Bernard's involvement in Europe has him writing them often.

Some of his buddies tried hunting the wild goats on his island. Les says he'd rather not go with them, as some of the greenhorns don't know one end of the gun from the other. He definitely didn't like how they barbecued what they shot.

December 30th's letter tells about going to Mass and praying that his brothers knew when to run when the Germans swept into their midst in the Battle of the Bulge. He was left behind with a few others as his old squadron shipped out.

January is full of anxiety for the family, Les, far around the world included. News of Bernard's wound, Paul and Vincent missing in action hit hard. Les holds out hope that Vincent's thunderbolt fighter would withstand a lot and he may have been able to bail out. February meant another month of anxiety, but also good news that his sister Hestel had married on February 3rd.

Hestel and Doug

By February 19th he's heard that Vincent was alive, though captured. He prays for the same for Paul. Les is re-transferred to Oahu.

March 18th and the news Paul was alive, but captured has everyone, (including his older brother) breathing easier. Bernard is back in a hospital in the US. Les enjoys a five-day pass to another island. The first time he's been off for more than 12 hours.

April brought news of FDR's death, a blow to all. Les says many GI's couldn't remember another president. By the 30th the Browns had heard from Paul, but not Vincent. May brought news of Paul's prison being rescued after four months of his imprisonment. Mr. Briscoe sent a picture of Bernard at the Fort Bliss Hospital. Jeanne, in nursing school, contemplates joining the WACS or the WAVES, and asks Les why Mom and Bernard are dead set against the idea. After a short explanation he states, "You can mark me down as being against it, too."

Finally in June, word came of Vincent's camp being released from the Russians. Still concerned, he hopes Paul returns to the States soon.

As the war comes to an end, June and July letters talk about points needed for discharge, and more ranch news. He talks about his father's partnership with Charles Voight. Expressing concern for his father's possibly overtaxing the arid land with too many beeves; he talks about having "a steer for every bush!"

On July 8th, his letter comments on his sister Norma's expected baby. The Brown women at that time had a tradition of giving birth to boy/girl/boy/girl. He wagers Norma will have a girl following Bill's birth two years before. She did.

July 25th letter discusses Paul's impending discharge. He hopes Vincent, now restored to active duty, won't have to fly combat in the Pacific. Throughout his service time, baseball has been his favorite pastime, he remarks on tournaments, competition between units. He also enjoys watching major leaguers like Joe DiMaggio, McCormick, and Lodigiani play.

By September 4th, 1945 he celebrates Macarthur signing the Japanese peace treaty, and then speculates on his circumstance, a 37 year old being high priority for discharge. Best of all, Briscoe is getting back his land from the gunnery range.

October's letter tells of getting a visit from Father Diehl's brother. Long time Batesville pastor and friend to all the Browns, Father Diehl served in South Texas for decades.

On October 2nd, he is at the embarkation port, hoping for departure within days. Even then thinking of his family, he speculates on Paul's discharge.

Les gave 3-1/2 years to his country. He worked at the Briscoe ranch the rest of his life.